DEATH
& Continuing On

A Primer in Interdimensionality

ALSO BY SUSAN MORGAN

 *The Power of Dreams:*

Dream Tools for Navigating Your Life

 *The Mystic Dream Journal*

DEATH

& Continuing On

A Primer in Interdimensionality

Susan L Morgan

To: Karen

The Best Book Seller in the World! Thanks so much!

Love, S

2013

Mystic Dream Publishing House

P. O. Box 3213

East Hampstead, NH 03826

Text Design: Susan Morgan

Cover Photo: John McNally

Editor: Lee Moore, Jr.

ISBN-13:978-1481923125

First paperback printing, January 2013
ISBN-10:1481923129

This book is lovingly dedicated to

All who came before Us

and

My Mother Estelle

When I was but a small child,

unable to yet read,

you gave me a mountains worth

of lined paper,

and encouraged me to write books.

Table of Contents

Part Two

Forward

I was all but finished with this book, when I spontaneously remembered the deal I made with the Angel of Death fifteen years ago. I write in the first chapter of how I begged to have my life extended. I said it might be a good idea now to remember just *what* that deal was, as I had long forgotten. I was cavalier and did not give it another thought; till two weeks ago when it popped into my mind, as I stood in my kitchen mindlessly washing dishes. It was not a welcome reminder because I had asked the Angel to extend my life till my youngest was eighteen. I wanted to raise my children. I needed to raise my children! It is now just six months till my youngest is eighteen.

I have just been to the doctor for pain in my arm and it turns out to be a pinched nerve. While there, I also mention an unusual birthmark that has just cropped up right at the spot where the pain is. The doctor wanted to biopsy it, since she suspected it might be melanoma. She cut a four inch incision in my right arm to take this tiny birthmark and finished it with seven stitches.

I wasn't nervous about the biopsy, till I saw the incision the next day, while changing my bandage. Why would she need to make such a big incision unless she was pulling out much more than a tiny birthmark? I quickly went online and saw that if I had melanoma and they had to go deep to get it out, I had about six months left to live…the time till my sons eighteenth birthday and my allotted time from my life extension. (I realize that it is not a good idea to get important health information from the internet!)

I fell into a slump waiting for the results of my

biopsy. I bemoaned the irony of just finishing this book about Death. I also wondered if this was the result of my sometimes non- challant attitude towards speaking with the departed; maybe this was a punishment for not be respectful enough. As I moped about for days, I watched more television that normal, and every movie seemed to be about Death. I could not shift my attention away from it. I was facing my Death.

I told almost no one because I did want to deal with the potential emotional outflow. I would wait till I knew affirmatively either way. I know an inordinate amount of healers and psychics. I asked no one for help…yet. I am also able to facilitate healing, yet did not try so for myself. The problem was I was in a funk. I was not completely motivated to live! I found this appalling. I found my reaction appalling. Was I depressed? No. Was I suicidal? No. I only knew that if my body was giving up, I was not going to battle cancer. (I do not judge people that do battle cancer. I applaud them and their courage) I did not want to lose my hair. I was mortified by my own shallowness. I did not want to put in the energy required to fight cancer. I know where I am going when I cross, and it is glorious. I am also leaving tons of artwork I created, three books I have written, gardens I have grown, thousands of people I have taught dreamwork (some of them are very gifted) and my three children are awesome. A couple of people that knew my situation replied, "You can't go! You have more work to do!" My mind agreed completely, but not my heart. I now know firsthand *that it is my heart that keeps me here*. I spent days in and out of meditation, happily traveling to the other side.

At one point my deceased mother came through and interrupted my peaceful reverie while meditating, waving her arms fervently back and forth and shaking her head. She blocked me from continuing on my vision. She said, "You are not to leave now! Stop it! Stop traveling over here right now! Do not listen to the Doctor and take her word as truth."

I was still disappointed in myself that I could not rally the battle cry to live. That is till I had to go to court one Tuesday. A young man broke into our home almost a year ago and his court date finally came up; and it was planned that I would speak at his court sentencing as the victim in the crime.

I dressed and got ready on an especially cold morning in New Hampshire and arrived at court a few minutes late, and less than enthusiastic. His case was the first heard, and after a brief statement by the Judge, I was asked to go forward and speak my peace. I walked to the front of the packed court and out of my mouth came fifteen minutes of rage and anger towards someone that would steal from me, but more importantly stole from my youngest son. Most of the items stolen were my sons; things that he paid for himself since he has worked since he was fifteen. My son's truck had all his windows smashed and was declared totaled by his insurance company just a few weeks back (we know) from this same young man. The young man's parents stood in the back sneering at me, to the point that armed guards had to stand next to them. (The guards stayed with them until I left the building)

I started by announcing that my son asked me not to speak as my car would be next. But I would not allow him to bully our family anymore. I urged the Judge to consider sending him to a class on bullying. I told the court this young robber needed empathy, something he clearly lacked. The Judge agreed and since he clearly did not learn this from his parents (verified by their current behavior in court), the State of New Hampshire would teach it to him, as well as respect; that this is what is required when parents choose not to.

(I am not saying every person's behavior is the result of good or bad parenting. Also, talk is cheap, and in the this case the Judge gave him but four days incarcerated, two years' probation and some counseling. In my case, the scales of justice were not balanced)

But what happened as I walked out of the court is priceless; I felt a wave of fire rise up through me and my body and life became re- animated. I was 100% on this side of the veil and now quite anchored in my body. The half of me that is Scots Irish kicked in and my fight was back, and with that, also my life. I was back to fight the 'good fight.'

When I got home, I had a sense the doctor would get my biopsy results that day, though I was told it wouldn't be for a few more days. I called and left a message that if the results came in, to please give me a call. At the end of the day they called to say that I do not have cancer. I was very relieved. I also knew that since I had decided to live earlier in the day, that it helped determine my biopsy results. If I had remained apathetic on whether I wanted to live or not, I would have had cancer.

How can I say such an irrational thing? From experience. I was told once that I wasn't pregnant when I went to get prenatal vitamins. I knew I was pregnant even though I had not missed my period. (intuition) The lab work came back negative and I told the nurse I knew I was pregnant and please just give me the pre natal vitamins. She would not and I walked outside to my car. As I was getting in my car, the nurse rushed out the door shouting "You are pregnant! The color just changed while it sat atop the trash can!" Another time I broke my ankle. I went to the hospital and they took x-rays. They came back that I did not have a break. I knew I did and said so. (intuition again) As I turned to leave, another doctor came and told me he read the x-ray and I did have a break. Sometimes we know more than the ‘experts’. In a round about, ironic, spiraling sort of way, my life was extended by a robber. The robber that came into my home, fueled my desire to live. I was not robbed of life, but gifted life by a robber.

I had an aggressive form of cancer and now do not, because I chose life and God decided I am eligible for some more time. As a reminder that my life has been extended, I have a four inch scar on my arm, which a friend said looks like the Tree of Life!

Introduction

Why is the only thing guaranteed to happen in our life still a mystery? We traveled with Death at our side at the moment of our birth. (even while in utero) Hand in hand, it follows us along, a Silent Partner, witness to our entire life, moment by moment. Yet, we cannot see it, touch it, taste it, smell it, or feel it. It stands with us and *around* us. This is so fantastically amazing and made even more so, because we don't have a clue about it. The ancient *Tibetan Book of the Dead* had a horrible and frightening explanation for Death:

The Good Spirit, who was born simultaneously with you, will come now and count out your good deeds with white pebbles; and the Evil Spirit, who was born simultaneously with you, will come and count out your evil deeds with black pebbles.

Thereupon you will be greatly frightened, awed, and terrified, and will tremble; and you will attempt to tell lies, saying, "I have not committed any evil deed." Then the Lord of Death will say, "I will consult the Mirror of karma." He will look in the Mirror, wherein every good and evil act is vividly reflected. Lying will be of no avail.

Then one of the executive furies of the Lord of Death will place a rope around your neck and drag you along; he will cut off your head, extract your heart, pull out your intestines, lick up your brain, drink your blood, eat your flesh, and gnaw your bones; but you will be incapable of dying. Although your body be hacked to pieces, it will revive again. The repeated hacking (symbolizing the pangs of the deceased's conscience) will cause intense pain and torture. Even at the time that the pebbles are being counted out, be not frightened; tell no lies; and fear not the Lord of Death.

Your body being a mental body is incapable of dying even though beheaded and quartered. In reality, your body is of the nature of voidness; you need not be afraid. The Lords of Death are your own hallucinations. Your desire-body is a body of propensities, and void. Voidness cannot injure voidness; the qualityless cannot injure the qualityless. Apart from one's own hallucinations, in reality there are no such things existing outside oneself as Lord of Death, or God, or Demon. Act so as to recognize this.

Things we don't know or understand are often feared. I imagine, just like our personal God, we each have a personal Death of sorts. Mine is merciful and gracious, angelic in every sense of the word. Perhaps if your God is wrathful, so is your Death companion. My God is ever-flowing with Love and abundance, and that pretty much sums up my Angel of Death.

I have come to this awareness in a couple of ways; contemplation and experience; well, as much experience as can be gained while I am still alive. The only 'experts' are our Ancestors, and even then, there is room for misunderstanding as we will see.

The concept of dimension is not restricted to physical objects. High-dimensional spaces occur in mathematics and the science; these are abstract spaces, independent of the physical space we live in.

We exist simultaneously in multiple dimensions and across time, and I make a humble attempt in this book to shine light on this concept; that cannot be understood without adding death into the equation. My goal in this collection of my ramblings about Death is to share what I have seen and learned and perhaps inspire you to make a conscious effort to have a relationship with the companion that has not left you for even one breath. *Maybe Death lives in the momentary space between our breaths*; that feels right.

Chapter One

No Date for Death

The whole life of man is but a point of time; let us enjoy it.

Plutarch

I have had Death brush by my cheek more than once. It might be that all of us have. The thing that strikes me most about each time this has happened to me is that I am unafraid. I am unafraid of crossing over, yet very afraid of what I may be leaving behind.

Crazy Man

I had a loaded gun held to my head by a crazed man on drugs. I was more concerned how I was going to get my six month baby out of the house than I was with dying. I was *not* going to let my infant son grow up without his mother. So when the killer found his bladder needed emptying, I was graced ninety seconds, and was able to grab my baby from his crib and run outside to my car. My baby on my lap, I quickly started the car and pushed the button to close my driver's window. Too late; the killer got to me with my window still open an inch. He shoved his fingers into that inch and pulled the entire window out of the car; glass shattering everywhere. Simultaneously, I slammed the car into reverse and left.

Tippy Canoe

Another time I fell out of a canoe on a sunny day in April. The sun was warm, but the water in Long Island Sound was ice cold. My friend and I yelled and waved but to no avail. We stopped struggling after a few minutes and became concerned about other things. For my friend, her gaze never left the watch on my left wrist and how it was going to be forever ruined. 'Such a lovely watch to be ruined' she thought over and over. My own attention was on an island, *Little Dumpling*, a few hundred yards off. I kept thinking it belonged to a TV character from the sixties television series *Gilligan's Island.* I was not thinking I wanted to go there, only what a sweet island it was. A fishing boat from the seaside town of Noank, CT saw us and rushed to our rescue. When they asked us to climb aboard, we both just looked at them incredulously. Neither of us could feel our bodies. As they hauled us up, my friend announced she would not talk to the press… (which there was no press obviously.) I thanked them and told them I would bake them a cake… (which I never did unfortunately.) We were both hallucinating and moments from Death. We were not worried, and rather calm.

Angel Shouts

One afternoon, on my way home from taking my youngest to his pre- school class, I had another brush with Death. I sat at the light of a mildly busy intersection waiting for the light to turn green. As soon as it did I drove forward, but within ten feet or so I heard a loud "STOP!" as if a man was in my car with me. I was so startled, I slammed on my brakes right in the middle of the intersection. As I did, I saw an elderly man drive past the front of my car, unaware he just drove through a red light. If I had not had an angel yell stop I would have been hit 'dead on' my driver's side.

Angel of Death

I have had pneumonia four times in my life. The last was the worst since I had double pneumonia as well as a viral infection. I laid on the couch for a couple of weeks, too weak to do anything at all; I was using a breathing machine which kept me one step ahead of death. I could hardly talk let alone walk. I should have been in the hospital. One night, it was Open House for my daughter's kindergarten class. This annual event is when the parents go to the school to meet the teacher and see all the work the children have created. There is always a letter to the parents created by the child on their little desk. It is a highlight of parenting for me and my heart broke that I was unable to go. That night while everyone was at the school, and as I lay on the couch, eyes closed, I sensed a tall being come next to me. It felt female and angelic. I started to weep, thinking, *"Oh God, now I have an Angel of Death standing here."* I started to implore the angel, "*Please do not take me now! Who will raise my children? My youngest is just two and needs me! My daughter needs me! My oldest son needs me! You don't need me in heaven, I am needed here! God, listen to me! Don't make me go with her! I will give back in my life if you let me live. What I will give I do not know, but I will think of something, and I will be a loving mother to these sweet children!"* (It might be worth me trying to remember what I promised!) The Angel smiled and gently touched my face. She pulled back and as she did, she told me that it was my choice that time. She also told me that there will be a total of seven times in my life when I will have a choice to stay or leave. Then she was gone.

Quarry Drowning

I stood on the edge of a beautiful cliff, part of a bowl shaped rock formation surrounding a little known, local, quartz crystal quarry. The water below was exquisite. I noticed for the first time how light plays along water; changing from specks of light on the shadows of dark to specks of dark on light. I was mesmerized. I was also young and impulsive. I stripped down to nothing and jumped off the cliff in a perfect swan dive. Half way into my descent, my innocence left, fear gripped me and I thought how I really was not a diver! My body changed immediately into a falling discombobulation of arms and legs and hair. I hit the water hard and all wind was knocked out of me. I sunk deep into the water, and as I did, time slowwwwed. Panic for air was quickly replaced by surrender as I realized I could never make it back to the top of the water in time, my body now a rock. Suddenly, I was at the top of the water gasping for air. I do not remember rising; I had been pushed up. I knew an angel had a vested interest in my life in that moment.

I am inclined to think there may have been more times as well. Either I am not remembering them right now, or perhaps it happened and I 'dodged the bullet' so to speak, unaware of the divine protection I received. I know I had my heart broken so bad once that my life thread connecting me to my body was all but severed. We have all heard stories of a person passing just days after their life long spouse passes. A broken heart can do that. I know how this feels, and we are alive more on a voluntary basis than most of us are aware. I know how to travel to the realm of the departed; it is a familiar road now and maybe I will take myself there at the end of my days, if I am graced with the choice.

Chapter Two

My Mother is Dying

I just realized that there's going to be a lot of painful times in life, so I better learn to deal with it the right way.
Trey Parker and Matt Stone, South Park, Raisins, 2003

We knew she was going to be crossing over soon. She was losing her three year battle with lung cancer. The cancer was also in her brain and no matter how valiant her effort in staying alive, Death was now on the winning side. It was close to Christmas and watching the agony of my father taking care of the woman he adored for close to forty five years of marriage was almost as hard to witness as my mother's passing. Everything about this hurt my heart; deeply. My own three children were young and I did not want to subject them to my intense grief. I allowed myself about fifteen minutes a night (a week or two before her actual passing) to do what I termed 'The Italian Woman Grieving." I am not Italian. I would go upstairs to a bedroom and throw myself on the floor and wail from the bottom of my heart. After this purge, I would wash my face and go back downstairs and resume family life. My children knew I was sad and had been crying and that my mother was dying, but I protected them (and myself) from a public display of my anguish. Though my mother and I were as different as oil and water, I still spoke with her every day, from wherever I was… *every day of my life.* I could not conceive of my life without her and her dry sense of humor.

A week before her death she went into a coma. I went to visit and sat beside her. I remembered reading that our sense of hearing is the last to go, so with that in mind, I took a gamble that she might still be able to hear me. I talked about everything large and small with her while she lay motionless on her bed. At one point I said, *"Now Mom, don't worry about Paul (my older brother) getting meatpies (a French Canadian dish we always had on Christmas and*

New Year's) from you on Christmas, I will make him some like you always did." With this, she turned her head which had not moved in days, towards me, opened her eyes and said firmly, "Don't you dare cook him meatpies! He can cook his own from now on!" Stunned, I whispered back, "*Okay.*" She turned her head back and closed her eyes; forever. If she said anything after that to anyone else in the family, I am unaware of it. She pulled herself out of a coma to say her last words; basically don't cook for my brother! (Don't baby him) How funny and amazing!

I knew the day she was going to die. We all had a sense of this. That morning, I could not drag myself out of bed to see her. I knew it was non-sensical; but I reasoned if I did not get out of bed, I would not see her and then she would not die. My friend Dorine called and told me to get out of bed or she was coming over to drag me out of it. I knew she meant it, so I got myself ready for the dreaded day. I prayed on my hour drive to see my mother. My father answered the door looking a couple of steps from death himself. I went and sat next to my mom and held her hand; my hand looking just like her hand in shape and size, was surreal. Only, her hand turned blue as I held it for two hours. My mother always said I talked non- stop and fast my whole life. That day was no different. I talked about everything hoping she could hear me like she did the week before in her comatose state. I sang songs to her. I read from the Bible. I forgave her. I asked her forgiveness. I promised her everything I could think of. I begged her to just let go and not worry about any of us. "*Just let go Mom, it's okay. I promise we will do our best and be fine.*" At this point the hospice worker came in and said, "Do not talk like that! You don't know what you are saying. She will be dead a very long time; there is no rush."

"*I am not rushing my mother. I just don't want her to feel the need to hold on and stay strong for us anymore.*" Meanwhile my father was coming and going in the bedroom and also welcoming the steady stream of family arriving and waiting in the living room. They were holding their own quiet vigil. Normally they are the noisiest people on Earth, but now they sat in whisper quiet. I let go of my mother's blue hand, stood up and told her I was going to say hi and see who exactly was out in the living room. As I sat next to my favorite aunt, my father went into the bedroom and sat next to his wife. We heard him start to sing softly the love songs that they both always loved. My heart almost burst from the sweetness of it. (I would love to have love songs sung to me as I pass over. How different than the way most of us are subjected to face our Death. Let's all have an agreement that we sing love songs to each other if we are able, okay?) Suddenly my Dad yelled, "She is passing now I think!" My younger brother, my mother's younger sister Leona and I ran into her room. Her breathing had been 'the death rattle' for some time already (a phenomenon common when we are dying, a deep rattily sound not easily forgotten) but her breathing was now slowed to almost nothing at all. No sound. No movement. As we stood surrounding her bed, Leona welling with emotion, choked out, "Estelle let go and let your next breath be His." And with those words my mother heaved her last breath and I saw her Spirit rise out of her and float off to a corner of the room and leave through the ceiling. We all yelled in celebration. She did it! I felt as though I had witnessed a birth more than a death. Those sitting in the living room did not quite understand our excitement. For the next hour I busily cooked for my children, who were hours overdue for a meal. I also encouraged them to go and see their grandmother and touch her. We phoned family and friends and told them she had just died.

The hour following her death was a high. The time following that was not. Though it has been said so many times it is now cliché, it still is true; they are fine, we are not and have to learn to live without the people we have loved. How? I guess one day at a time. They come to us in dreams though, and my mother has come through many times, always with practical information. I am also able to connect with her sometimes in a conscious way. She was accessible while alive and is still pretty accessible and doing just fine too!

Chapter Three

Ancestral Memory

One of the advantages of being disorderly is that one is constantly making exciting discoveries.

A. A. Milne

When I was in England, I happened to take myself to London. While walking in downtown London, I came across a large building called Westminster Abbey and liked the look of it; massive and gray it looms over the entire block, and lined upon its arched doors are statues of saints and more, one atop the other. I had heard the name of this place before but that is all I knew. I walked thru the huge wood cathedral doors and within a moment my knees buckled. I was compelled to kneel and say a prayer before I entered any further. I was welled up with emotion for hours while I wandered throughout this enormous stone edifice to God, past Kings and Queens and the sacred burial place of so many artists and historical figures over the past thousand years. I could not explain my attraction, or strong emotion. I spent the entire day there, alone, and it went by in the blink of an eye. I remember standing in front of the wax figures and death masks of some of the former queens and kings of England, daydreaming of the lives each had led. I was both repulsed and fascinated.

Years later, an aunt would do the genealogy on my fathers' side of the family, and lo and behold, I am a descendant of the people that built Westminster, as well as many of the royalty buried there. My knees buckled when I had entered the Cathedral because my DNA recognized my connection to this place and people. Not a past life, but my genetic coding responded to something that my brain would not comprehend.

We have the blood and coding of our ancestors pumping through us. Very little changes genetically and we would do ourselves a favor if we recognized, in a physical way, the impact of our ancestry. We would renew the ancient practices of remembering our departed and sending them our love and prayers. We are woven and netted together in ways that do not recognize the march of time. Our bodies hold memories of people long forgotten.

Chapter Four

Roch Mantoueabeouichit

The path to our destination is not always a straight one. We go down the wrong road, we get lost, we turn back. Maybe it doesn't matter which road we embark on. Maybe what matters is that we embark.

Barbara Hall, Northern Exposure, Rosebud, 1993

I am instructed to lie down, along with thirty other people on the carpeted floor of a re-purposed monastery that rambles along the Sound of Long Island. Quiet nuns, and nun types, pad through the halls cleaning and preparing for the next meal as soon as the previous one is done and cleaned up; an endless cycle of domesticity. A tall Australian with a head of snow hair, stands holding a frame drum. He looks as though he might belong in a university teaching, but he has instead chosen a path that involves beating a drum like an indigenous person. He is my teacher of Dreamwork and despite all his quirkiness (he must have pockets and suitcases filled with quirkiness I imagine), I find him magnetic in his teaching. So I lie down and endeavor to reach an ancestor in the land of the dead and hope that I have access to this through the land of my imagination. I am somewhat doubtful they will intersect.

I lay with my eyes closed, a blanket pulled up to my chin, a notebook and pen lays next to me, at the ready, so that as soon as the trance inducing drumming stops, I will take notes on my experience. I do this so that I can retain all the information I will perceive. I have done this before and know all too well how it may wisp away like a dream if I do not pin it down to paper. Grab it and pin it.

As the drumming starts I say a silent prayer that only the most helpful of my ancestors come through please. I don't have the time and inclination to interact with any that may be dysfunctional. Of course dysfunctional can be construed as subjective, especially in my family!

With the steady heartbeat drumming in the background of my awareness, it disappears and my focus is replaced by me standing on the sandy shore of a point touching the ocean, the tips of my toes in the water. Immediately a whale swims up to me and in a friendly manner, grabs me by my toes and places me, in my entirety, at the front of his head. He swims me fast across the ocean towards an island I can see in the distance…maybe a few miles away. I don't question any of this or how it could happen. I am in the land of imagination and I know this can be a place of greater truth then the one in which I usually operate.

I expect to be greeted by a great number of relatives, but can see as the whale and I approach the island, there is a lone figure waiting to receive me. He is none too tall and could actually be described as small and wiry. I am starting to feel crestfallen. Gracefully, I am placed on this new beach by my aquatic burden bearer. As I face the mocha skinned man, whose eyes are lit up and smiling at me warmly, I try to hide my disappointment from him. Maybe he will take me to the others who must be waiting to embrace me. But no one else shows nor am I to meet anyone else. It is me and him, meeting the first time across many generations. He says, "I am your great grandfather Roch Mantoueabeouichit ." (He is actually many greats back in generations) I know who he is now but say nothing, yet.

He says; "Come!", and leads me inland a couple of hundred yards. We stop and sit on our haunches. "I want to show you how we ate", he says brightly. He picks up a clean clam shell and scoops up blueberries that appear from nowhere particular. "I am going to show you how to cook them!" (I am thinking; "*Why....I have a lot of questions and none of them include cooking!"*) He places the filled clam shell on a rock very close to a small fire. *Did this fire just appear or do I not notice it before?* Within a few minutes he hands me the warmed blueberries.

"They are delicious. Try them!"

I do, and he is right, they are sweeter than sweet, but not mushy like pie. I vaguely remember something I had heard about eating in the land of the dead, and hope I have not just incurred long time damage of some sort to my Soul. I trust this man though, even if he looks unfamiliar. There is nothing sinister in his demeanor. He is gentle and appears to be aware of my cautiousness, and is patiently amused by me and my cynicism.

"We cook the blueberries just to the point before they burst. It releases the sugar in them and makes them delicious. No? We made jokes about the size of a clam shell one would use. The greedier a person, the bigger their clam shell. No one wanted a really big clam shell and to be perceived this way. We used the clam shell as a spoon, bowl, or serving tool."

"Thank you, but could you please tell me why you gave your only daughter to the French to be trained in White Man's ways knowing she was also going to be married to a White Man in their customs?" I say this trying to hide any judgment in my voice.

"Oh yes, we will talk about that but first let me show you how we cook fish!"

I am growing impatient and realize I have a precious few minutes to get family information before the drumming stops. Where are the others? Why am I not meeting my mother who is in this realm? I am not that interested in cooking.

I have issues with why this man gave up his daughter. I read about this, years back in the Jesuit Relations; a compilation of books written by French missionary priests trying to convert 'savages' to Christianity during the early years of contact between the two peoples. Though the books are clearly biased and racist, they also offer a glimpse of the culture of natives if one can read through the cloudiness of the subjective reality of the Jesuits. Both Roch and his Huron wife Outchibahabanoukoueou , gave up both their children. The Jesuit Relations say of the son:

DEATH AND CONTINUING ON

From the Jesuit Relations 1635. My Huron Ancestors:

On the 14th of the same month, we baptized in our Chapel at Kebec, with the holy ceremonies of the Church, a little child a few months old; its parents had named it Ouasibiskounesout, and Monsieur Gand called it François. This poor little one was very sick, but God soon afterwards restored it to health. It's father's name was Mantoueabeouichit, and its mother's, Outchibahabanoukoueou.

... But to return to our little François. When his parents came back from the woods in the early Spring, Monsieur Gand, who is as charitable as

possible to these poor barbarians, recognized his little godson; calling him by name, this poor little fellow answered him falteringly, but in so pretty a way,—he is indeed a very beautiful child,—that Monsieur Gand straightway had a little dress made for him in the French fashion. As soon as he shall be in a condition to be taught, I hope we shall get him for instruction; his father and mother promised this when he was baptized.

Later they speak of how little Francois kept running away as a child, refusing to be trained. He ended up back home with his parents and larger family. I am also aware the Natives had to baptize their children or risk having them killed intentionally or via disease. With the baptism came the promise the parents would let their Native children grow in devotion to the white man's God. The Settlers made every point to the Natives that their God was greater than the 'savages' God.

The White Settlers changed the name of my great, great grandmother, daughter of Roch Mantoueabeouichit and Outchibahabanoukoueou, from Ouchistauichkoue to Marie Sylvestry.
(Sylvestry meant 'from the woods")

She was placed with the Ursaline nuns in Quebec City, Canada and taught French, White Man's prayers, wore White Man's clothes and taught all manner of a White Man's life. Perhaps because she was a girl, she accommodated them all. She was allowed to visit her parents from time to time but was always sent back. The Jesuits said of this;

...They have given one of their children, a little girl, to sieur Olivier, who cherishes her tenderly; he provides for her, and is having her brought up in the French way. If this child occasionally goes back to the Cabins of the Savages, her father, very happy to see his daughter well clothed and in very good

condition, does not allow her to remain there long, sending her back to the house where she belongs. ...

This is what I needed to understand! Not cooking!

As if in response to my thoughts, Roch Mantoueabeouichit, replies; "We will talk about that. First you need to know how we cooked. How we lived. This is important so that our culture can live on and not be stolen from us."

My attitude and impatience are softened by this comment.

"We would find a nice plank of wood; preferably Maple and place it on rocks in the fire." He takes a foot long board of Maple and places it on the hot rocks. He then places a fish on it.

"That's it!" he smiles. "It won't take long to cook. And it is nothing to clean up after either!"

"I have something for you," he says. He hands me a shucked ear of corn about five inches long. "This is Abenaki corn."

I blurt, *" This can't be right. It is too short."*

"This is truly our corn and I want you to know this."

We are done with the cooking now and he is ready to discuss my other things with me. "With regard to my daughter; we loved her very much. That is why we gave her away. We knew that she would probably die if we kept her since so many of us were dying. The White People told us their Creator was greater than ours. We did not believe this, but why were we dying? The White People were not going to go back to where they came from. We had to get along. I was a leader of my tribe; a spiritual leader. Manitou in my name means White Spirit. The man I chose to let her go with was my friend, Martin Prevost. I had worked with him in the capacity of teaching him the survival methods we used. I trusted him more than most White People. He promised he would always take care of our daughter and he did. He was much kinder than most of the White Men to their wives. So see? I knew what the best choice was. He allowed her to come see us too. We were not allowed near the Ursaline nuns, nor in their community that they had built. They would not harm us, but it was understood for the peace of both sides, to recognize the boundary lines of our homes and to respectfully refrain from too much interference. The boundaries of the White Men were more important to them than anything else. All decisions related around issues with their boundaries; in land and in God.

It hurt our eyes and ears and noses too much to go near their villages often. They were always busy building a life. So much of what they found important we did not understand. We hoped we would gain understanding through our daughter. Her children, and the many generations following, would be protected too if their father was a White Man and she was married in their traditions. She was honored by becoming the first Native to marry a White Man and all the White People celebrated this; most of them anyways. They were married in the church Notre Dame in Quebec City. We did not attend but visited later in the day. The sun shone that day and birds were singing. We saw this as a blessing.

I saw Monsieur Prevost more than Marie after their wedding. I still worked with him often and Marie was busy raising eight children; my descendants. Monsieur Prevost let us send our daughter Native medicine when she was in labor giving birth. This was the only time they let us interfere with their customs. The fear of losing her during childbirth was great, especially so, after they had invested years training her to fit into their culture.

Would you like to meet Marie, your great, great grandmother?"

"Yes!"

Out from a spot near the fire, stepped a small woman. She was about 5' tall, small framed with thick black hair. She had large brown eyes that were soft and if there was a spark of light representing happiness, I could not find it. She was not sad, but rather had a look of earnest concern. Maybe that was just her expression since she was meeting me. She spoke not a word. She was waiting for me to speak first. I awkwardly said, "*Hello*". She smiled and gestured for me to step towards her. It was as though she did not possess the physical mobility that her father had in this realm. I took about ten steps and stood directly before her. I was slightly taller and fuller. Her face broke into a broad smile and she pulled me into her embrace, whispering some Native words tenderly. My eyes welled.

Softly she said, "You are mine too. My babies had you. I helped you find my grave when you looked." (I had gone to Quebec the previous year to find her grave as well as the school she was trained in, and the church she had been married in.) "Thank you for remembering me and our people. I was not sad with my father's decision and thought I was lucky that the French thought I was smart enough to train. My husband, Monsieur Prevost was a kind husband and took care of me and our children. Our children liked him very much.

They forgot much of our ways though and that was the plan. It was considered a successful experiment and this was in great part due to me and my abilities. Don't look at this as a bad thing or let it make you angry anymore okay? It was all planned and agreed to, and most people in that time did not have lives that were acceptable. I was lucky."

I silently nodded, stunned that I had misunderstood so deeply. I still did not like that they were forced to make the choices they did. My concerns were irrelevant a few hundred years later though and I now knew this.

Roch Mantoueabeouichit walked over to where we stood. He said to me, "Dear daughter, you do not know of my wife Outchibahabanoukoueou, Marie's mother. Another time we will talk about this but your time with us is up for now. I want you to know that I traveled to your great, great grandmother, and loved her very much. *I traveled true and I traveled strong. I traveled North to my true Love."*

His words stung at my heart as I heard them. 'I will travel North to my true Love' I thought and I will remain strong and true like my own mothers peoples.

"I have a gift for you as you go", he continued. He handed me a piece of the Abenaki corn.

I gave him a kiss and left.

The drumming that was out of my range of awareness for the previous fifteen minutes, was now loudly in the room. Moments later as it came to a stop, I forced myself to be in my body, on the floor in Connecticut, in this time and era.

The next day I am sitting at my desk and AOL's headline story is**: Ancient Abenaki Corn Found**. Under this is an image of the corn; five inches long and looking like the corn my ancestor gave me. I am stunned. The story goes on to say that the seeds have been held in New England for generations and the keepers of the corn have decided it is time to give it back to the Abenaki.

It is times like this that have taught me that there are dimensions and people accessible across time and space. *And it is this ability that lets me speak with the departed.*

Chapter Five

Tim

The most important thing she'd learned over the years
was that
There was no way to be a perfect mother
and a million ways to be a good one.
Jill Churchill

The first time I was aware I could clearly hear the departed came when I was in my early thirties. I found it frightening indeed.

I am seated at a long wooden table with strangers, except one. He is an old acquaintance I met in my travels, years back, in England. We are gathered at this dinner hour, somewhat formally, in his honor. He has flown across the pond, to be at this celebration of his exceptional marine art, in no small part due to me; or so he thinks. The restaurant is a few feet from the Mystic River in Mystic, CT. It is built of old beams and yellowing plaster. It holds us in a warm embrace as we await dinner; the smell of salt water permeating the air. The art gallery next door is associated with The Mystic Seaport, where this landmark restaurant is located, and is the opposite in its approach to its patrons. There is no warm embrace but rather a cool aloofness in the art gallery. It is assumed only the privileged will appreciate this art as well as have the ability to procure it. Most of the art is of seas and boats and dappled light. Boats most people have only seen in paintings, but do sail the wide seas of our globe. I met my English friend because of a boat, much like those in the surrounding paintings.

My boyfriend at the time (and future husband) was a custom racing yacht builder. I always wished there was a more succinct way to explain his profession, but all the descriptive words were required. He had built a fast, award winning boat (one of many) that was representing the United States in an international boat race called the Whitbred Race , that had been held on the Isle of Wight, (an island of the southern coast of England) annually for the past

150 years. We were housed in a four story mansion on the Isle of Wight along with twelve other couples and two French cooks; the crew of the yacht. The owner generously paid all expenses and even supplied plenty of clothes and foul weather gear etc., (all top of the line), in fitting with all the other yachts from across the globe racing at this event. Team outfits, creatively designed with speedy looking logos and graphics. These boats were the crème de la crème in racing yachts of various lengths; this is what the super-rich can do. I was poor, but that is irrelevant to the story really, and only worth mentioning as a counterbalance to all the excess. We also had, as our Captain, the infamous Ted Turner who happened to be on the cover of

Playboy that month. (In a windy way all this leads to a story about the departed if you will just stay with me and follow this thread!)

The twelve couples consisted of the men who were racing, along with their wives (sans children); to wave them back home from the dock at the end of each days race. My boyfriend and I were not married and since I was *only* a girlfriend, we were relegated to the attic rather than a well- appointed bedroom; the space which also housed the washer and dryer. The attic was huge and bright and very comforting.

I also had the habit of being late to the daily evening dock waving ritual, as if a cheerleader, and was scolded more than once because of this. In the late afternoon, the wives would wait in anticipation of their beloveds boat arriving. This is an old tradition and very sweet. They get the heads up of when the boats will be heading back to the dock via ship to shore radios. This was not exact, so plenty of time was spent with the women milling about the end of the dock discussing what wants to be discussed. I was an outsider. Young, pretty and more interested in painting my own little oil landscapes that summer, than bonding with wealthy married women I had nothing in common with other than that our men were racing sailors. As an aside, the most charming, handsome and fun loving men I have met were the professional yacht racers. The personality and physical skill required to be proficient in this arena is very attractive.

Back to Ted Turner; everyone in the house was a tither on whether to treat him like the rest of us; meaning small talk and socializing with us at every meal etc. There was also a Big Concern about the Playboy article, for which Ted's interview was the featured article that month, and I think he may have even been on the cover. Was it in good form to mention that we all knew this or should we pretend not to know? The latter was the adopted technique. The biggest obstacle with the Playboy article was that Ted had controversially referred to some women as cows. (at that time the word controversy and the name Ted Turner, whose nickname was The Mouth of the South, were always connected anyway) This was not acceptable language yet no one dared get in a conversation with him that might veer off into that direction. Ted also had brought with him his second wife Jane; all of Teds' wives have been named Jane. I am sure he has pondered that more than once. So the tone of the house would generally be light hearted and friendly, until either Jane or Ted walked in; and then a reserved hush could be palpably felt. No one really talked with either of them. Worse, the women completely scorned Jane and even went so far as to ridicule her behind her back; for reasons I cannot remember. (Really there was no good reason, because Jane was, above all else, lovely and gracious) It is best to think of these wives as high school cheerleader types, only older, and their clannishness was adolescent. I did not fit in, nor did I care to, and neither did Jane. I befriended Jane. She was grateful to say the least. Ted was grateful and told me so.

Each morning Jane would ask me what I was doing for an adventure that day and if she could join me. I preferred to be on my own to paint and wander about, but sometimes we would walk to town together. On one such occasion, we happened to walk into a small art gallery filled from floor to ceiling with marine art. It was stunning. I was completely enthralled with the tightness of the renderings as well as the grace of each painting. My loud enthusiasm spilled over and the creator of these paintings, along with his wife, stepped out from behind a curtain, apparently listening to us. We had a great time and later that day, when Ted came home from the race, Jane told him about our 'outing'. (She liked that word, and I found it amusing as if I had stepped back into summers in New Jersey in the 1940's-ish) She insisted he come see this artist and his work since I went crazy over it. As much to appease her as anything else, he went. I am told he exclaimed upon seeing the paintings; "This man is the next Van Gogh!" (which is comical since there is nothing familiar in the artist's technique to Van Gogh's) He proceeded to buy all the paintings and made arrangements to have them shipped to his offices in Atlanta. The artist, Tim Thompson, was already regarded as the official Marine Artist for England, but it was Ted Turner's patronage that propelled him to international fame.

A few years later, back in the scene with me sitting next to the honoree Tim Thompson, at a prestigious dinner, and synchronistically it is being held in my home town. I have not seen Tim in a few years though we have kept in touch via letters. We had an instant bond years prior when we met. He had shown me all around Cornwall, (the southern part of England), and introduced me to the most delicious and decadent food on Earth; clotted cream from Devonshire. I distinctly remember I knew then that I had known him from another life and in that same location of Cornwall. Time felt rubbery when I was with him.

At one quiet point of the dinner, as we awaited the serving of the entrée, Tim confides in me that his mother had recently passed. I extended my sympathies, and he mentions some small problems in his relationship with her, and continues to explain his version of their story. Suddenly, and without any warning, I blurts, "*No dear, you were mistaken on how I felt!*" his mother apparently channeling through me. She continues, telling her son who sat aghast next to me, how she would like to heal the past and desperately wanted him to know how very much she loved him. I am stunned, teary and a little embarrassed by my outburst and I can see Tim has tears in his eyes. I fumble as I admit I have never done this before, yet I know it was his deceased mom. Tim nods in agreement that it was her. It seems to me that the departed can pick up when someone (in this case me) can hear or see them, and often they want to communicate. Now, years later, I am often thanked by the people on 'the other side' while I do a reading.

Chapter Six

The Loving Husband

He is the half part of a blessed man,
Left to be finished by such as she;
And she a fair divided excellence,
Whose fullness of perfection lies in him.

William Shakespeare

I am sitting in a brightly lit room, every inch filled floor to ceiling with books. I am invited to this home by an elderly woman. She is stylishly poised; every detail of her home and herself is thoughtfully and artistically arranged. I am fascinated. She has asked me to come to her home for a private Dreamwork session. She had seen my name mentioned in *Dreamways of the*

Iroquois by Robert Moss and I realize she is 'testing' me as much as anything else. She shares with me that she has studied, in depth, Jung and Dreamwork. At that time, I had no knowledge of Carl Jung, and had only heard his name. She also told me that she had worked in a hospital setting in Texas with dying children. She was inspired to ask them their dreams and wrote them down, later giving them to the grieving parents after the child had passed. I was completely impressed by her generous spirit. Her approach to Dreamwork was analytical, mine is not, and hence where the testing came in.

I asked her to share a dream with me. She shared a dream of her departed husband. We talked a little about the dream and I asked her a few key questions to gain clarity about the possible meaning of the dream.

Drum a Dream

Robert Moss developed a technique he calls *Lightning Dreamwork* which is very effective in understanding dreams, especially our 'everyday' ones. But our bigger dreams, the ones that are not so easily forgotten, or the recurring, or the ones that have our departed loved ones require a deeper level of understanding that can best be accomplished by shamanic methods; drumming oneself into the dream. You don't have to be a shaman to work shamanically, we can all access information that can be easily acquired this way. It is experiential and I have not found the words yet to accurately convey this depth of experience. I usually just say, "*Let's do it.*"

Words fail us when we are describing a nonlinear experience. It is imagery and emotion that best serve our understanding on these things. It is why our dreams speak to us in imagery and emotion, not the written word.

Since her dream could be classified as a Big Dream, and she was curious about me and my drum, I decided to drum myself into her dream. This is done with me sitting with my large frame drum resting on my lap as I quietly tap it at a pretty fast pace with what is called the beater, or drum stick. It is known that when our brain hears a drum beat at approximately 180 - 200 beats per minute (in some cultures this is known as the Eagle's heartbeat, or heartbeat of Mother Earth) it naturally adjusts our brains waves to a state called theta, enabling us to enter the land of active imagination as well as access other dimensions and realms. But much like learning how to ride a bike, you have to feel your way into it. One cannot try to count the correct number of beats per minute to 'launch', because it is too much coordination. But, we can *feel* ourselves to the perfect rate of speed to give a jump to our consciousness.

I close my eyes, and start at the beginning of her dream. This is called the Dream Gate. I push my consciousness through her dream as I recalled her telling it to me, only now I can see her deceased husband and he is talking with me, as was not part of her dream. I am not surprised because this is what happens when we journey into a dream; more information spills forth and we can dialogue with any aspect of the dream that we desire. Her husband gives me specific information on his build (he was quite tall) as well as the nickname he called her. He had other information he wanted to convey in addition to his undying love for her. After approximately ten minutes of drumming I open my eyes and take a moment or two to adjust 'back.' I share what I have seen and heard with the Dreamer, uncensored. This dear woman, who normally functions with full composure, is now weeping. She confirms all the details as well as the sweet nickname he called her. She knows he has reached through the veil.

Chapter Seven

The Loving Father

It is a wise father that knows his own child.
William Shakespeare

I still did not make the connection that I connect with the departed easily. Another time I am at the funeral of my ex-husbands uncle. As we drive up to the cemetery for the burial I clearly see the deceased uncle standing, in his spirit form, near the gate to the headstones and his grave. He is joyous. He sees that I can see him, and we make direct eye contact. He tells me how happy he is with how the funeral is going. He goes into detail about some of the people attending and how much they meant to him, especially a couple of old friends that he had not seen in years. He then tells me his concerns for his daughter and shares what he would like her to do with his household items. He is also very concerned about her emotional state due to his death. I had only met this man a few times while he was alive, and though I instantly loved him, I knew little about him and nothing about his daughter. At the dinner, following the burial service, I debated whether I should share what happened with his daughter. We had never met and I did not want to come across as a nutcake, and even more I did not want to possibly add to her sadness. I remembered he had also said two Native words to me on the night that he passed. He came to me in spirit and said, "*Onan Kawanado*". I have looked up the meaning of his words and the closest I can find is in Mohawk the word *onen*: That's it, and kewenni:io (*gawonneeyo)*: I am free; hence '*That's it, I am free.*'

After we finish dessert, I walk over to his grown daughter and introduce myself. I add, that at the risk of her thinking I am crazy, I want to share my experience of her father's passing. She is grateful and acknowledges what I have seen. Later, she mails me a signed copy of a John Holland book, also a Medium who connects with the departed, and is a friend of hers! Who would have known!

(As an aside; many years after this experience, I move to New Hampshire and my office is in the quintessentially quaint town of Exeter, New Hampshire. After a number of months of being there, I learn that Dan Brown author of The Da Vinci Code, as well as other books, had his office just a few doors down from mine. I found this lucky somehow. Later again I learn that John Holland's office is two blocks the other direction yet on the same road; I am 'squished' between the two. Why does this matter to me? Because I am aware of things naturally happening in bunches; good things throughout history. I have a better chance of being a recognized writer (Dan Brown) or Medium (John Holland) than if I was stuck in some backwoods, only time will tell, and I certainly didn't plan it this way, but it has caught my attention. Whether any material gain ever comes to me or not, I feel better just being in the same vicinity as highly creative or gifted people!)

Chapter Eight

Death Comes Knocking

In prosperity our friends know us; in adversity we know our friends.

John Churton Collins

One late summer night, I had the strange inspiration to think about what I would do if my friend and roommate Cathy died. She had just come 'out of the closet' and in 1979 that was not a welcome thing, even by me at that time. I asked her to keep it under wraps and she agreed. She knew her aunt that raised her, as well as her birth mother, would not be supportive. Horrified would be a more likely response. Curiously, I went through a mental checklist of how I would distribute her humble belongings if she should ever pass, and then did not give it a second thought.

Until two weeks later when there was a knock on my front door at three in the morning. I woke to the knock and knew instantly what it meant. I went anxiously to the door and opened it. There stood a policeman. He asked me if any family of Cathy's were available. I replied she did not live with her family. I knew why he was there…I urged him to just spit it out. We stood with our eyes locked, unblinking; me begging him to tell me what I already knew and he telling me he was required to only talk with her family. Finally, I told him I was 'like family', and that was enough for him to confirm my friend Cathy had died in a freak car accident that evening by hitting a fire hydrant; which pushed the steering wheel into her chest. As if in a dream, he turned and walked away.

My boyfriend was sleeping over and upon hearing my conversation at the door, quickly dressed and ran to go out the back door. But not before I implored him to stay. He told me, incredulously, he could not stay because he felt now that Cathy was dead, she must know all the cheating he had done behind my back, and he feared her ghost! All this took place in a time of less than ten minutes. The shock of his confession paled in comparison to the news my friend had just passed. I could only process so much, so he received a couple of day's dispensation till I could regroup and confront him on that hurtful bit of info.

I was asked early that morning to go to the morgue to confirm it was her body. This was more than my nineteen year old self could handle and I refused. Mechanically, I took care of Cathy's belongings like I had 'seen' in my imagination two weeks before. I waited till eight in the morning and called her family and informed them of what happened. Her aunt later told me on the night Cathy passed; her childhood cat anxiously paced back and forth across the headboard of her old bed, meowing all night long. Cathy's cat sensed her death. There are many stories of animals that can sense death.

If everything is so good when we pass, as we will see later in this book, then what is the value of enduring a difficult and sometimes impossible life? We are not always privy to our larger story and I strongly believe we need to be here as long as we are supposed to be here… period. The collateral damage of a suicide is profound; rippling out to all who cared for the deceased is one primary reason. The departed also have the challenge of seeing the hurt caused by their untimely exit.

Did my friend commit suicide? No, but I always felt her desire to stay alive was not strong enough to block the accident from happening. I suspected her apathy allowed it. Every new roommate I had afterwards would complain there was a ghost in their bedroom, even though I made a point of not sharing my friends passing. Her spirit remained unsettled for quite a while.

Chapter Nine

Ghosts

History never looks like history when you are living through it.
John W. Gardner

There is a house in the old New England seaside town of Noank, CT that is renowned for being haunted. This is not hard to imagine if you see the house on a moonlit night in October. It looms over the landscape with towering spires. But during the day it takes on a charming look with its gingerbread bric- a- brac and a large farmer's porch. Ghost hunters from far and wide have come to this town for the explicit reason of seeing this house. Each owner has happily obliged these tourists and their curiosity. The Noank Historical Society says the house was built on a piece of land known as "Harry's Ledge" after a local resident, Harry Burrows. He sat on this high ground day after day looking out to sea - waiting for a ship that never came.

In 1884, Robert Palmer, the deacon of the Noank Baptist Church and owner of the Palmer Shipyard (the precursor to the Noank Shipyard) built the house at the height of the Victorian era. His employment of skilled cabinetmakers and shipwrights, together with access to materials sailed in from across the world in coastal schooners, allowed him to create an opulent Victorian home.

My old boyfriend wanted to buy it. It was two blocks from his shop at The Noank Shipyard (!) where he built boats and he envisioned housing multiple boat builders/employees with me cooking and running basically a boarding house. (Though unbeknownst to us at the time, it would have been a fitting use for the house.) This did not appeal to me for obvious reasons, but especially so, because the house was notorious for being haunted. He insisted on taking a tour of the house when it became listed for sale. A couple of friends volunteered to come along with us as well. I felt that if the house was in fact haunted, the ghost would know that I was able to sense it. Much like we are told not to act scared near an aggressive dog or they can 'sniff' you out (good luck with that, if the dog is so savvy, I don't have a chance of hiding my fears) the ghost will try to scare me; easily done at that point in my life. I cautiously entered the house with my friends and boyfriend, all of us in a line following the real estate agent. Everything was going well till we reached the third floor which was also the attic. The attic in an old Victorian is large and is actually another floor of usable living space, as this house had. As soon as we were climbing the narrow staircase to the attic I was filled with chills and dread. Just like I had heard somewhere, the air had actual cold pockets. I physically could not get to the top stair. Fear froze me as well as a sense of unexplainable oppression. I turned around, and trying to hold my composure, brightly told the others I would wait for them at the bottom of the staircase.

We finished our tour and I was relieved nothing of consequence happened. When we all reached the front door to leave, I turned to remark about the massive, five foot jade plant that was in a gorgeous ceramic planter, centered in front of the, floor to ceiling, bay window.

The planter came up to my knees. I walked over to get a better look at the planter, when all of a sudden the entire plant (more like a small tree) tipped over and landed at my feet. Nothing broke. I, along with everyone else, screamed. We ran out of the house, and even the real estate agent refused to go back in. The owners would have to clean up the mess. There was no way one person could have moved that heavy planter by themselves, let alone tip it over for no 'good reason.' The rumors were always that it was a sea captains ghost and I sensed he was a cranky one. Maybe he had a sense of humor, and seeing my barely veiled fear, thought it would be entertaining to give me a fright.

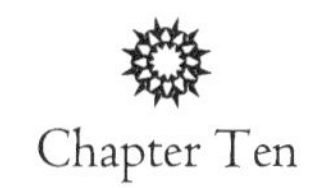

Chapter Ten

Whaling Ship

Look not mournfully into the past. It comes not back again. Wisely improve the present. It is thine. Go forth to meet the shadowy future, without fear.
Henry Wadsworth Longfellow

On a field trip with my youngest sons' elementary school to the Mystic Seaport Museum we all stopped to climb aboard the *Mystic Whaler*, a carefully restored whaling ship from the whaling days of the late 1800's. Our tour guide pointed to a small cabin- like building attached to the middle of the deck, it was primarily windows of glass. She informed us that this was where the captains' wife would stay on the long voyages at sea.

I 'saw' a scene that showed a woman, (not the captains' wife, nor anyone's wife), but rather a female whose purpose was to keep company with the men of the ship. I 'saw' how when she was in this very visible space it was a message for the crew to leave her alone. They could watch, but they could not touch. She was a caged bird. Maybe our tour guide already knew this but it was not considered suitable for a child to hear, I do not know. I do know what I 'saw' though. We can sometimes see layers of the past happening over the present time.

Time is Simultaneous

Old lives and stories are layered over the dimension we are aware of. Future lives may be as well. With second sight, we can see any number of stories layered over any piece of land on this Earth. Quantum physics now understand what shamans have known all along*; all time is simultaneously in the Now.* We have access to all and anything that has happened. Now doesn't that ramp up our responsibility for anything we create?!

Chapter Eleven

Unwelcome Visitor

How comes it, that thou art then estranged from thyself?
William Shakespeare

"Wake up!" yelled my then husband frantically. He was running back and forth across our bedroom floor, his eyes wide in panic. I could not, for the life of me, imagine what he was doing. "Don't you hear that?" he cried. I sat up and heard a low grumbling, growl-like sound. It sounded otherworldly and not at all friendly. "Do something!" he implored.

"*What can* I *do*?" I squealed in a worried whisper.

"I don't know but I think you could fix this! At least try!"

This bizarre event was happening after a month of almost nightly nonsense. The smoke alarms would go off in the middle of the night, and my ex-husband would run upstairs to check things out and turn them off. As he would turn off one, another would go off. These were battery run smoke detectors and none of it made sense, but my ex looked like a fool running around turning off the smoke detectors nightly; and it was exhausting.

I agreed to try. Lacking any training in ghost removal, I improvised what I thought might be the process. I grabbed a crucifix, a nice big one. I had some holy water from my great grandfather that somehow I had acquired in a small plastic bottle, and I grabbed that too. I got my oversized white Bible and placed it on the boat bar. (My ex had restored the back end of a 1952 Chris Craft that we first used as a bar, but when that proved needless, we converted it to my desk, the computer placed over the small sink. This was also in our bedroom. It was a big room with two huge windows looking out onto the lake, so I guess the back end of a boat was not completely out of context. Nor the painted wooden fish that were tucked in the cross beams!)

I sprinkled the holy water about, holding the crucifix in front of me, as I stood holding the Bible and said The Lord's Prayer aloud; all my Catholic upbringing in full force. I then asked for help from God, and a host of heavenly angels. (Why ask for one when we can have a host?) I then proceeded to talk aloud to a spirit hoping and assuming he could hear me. I had nothing to lose. I am talkative by nature and my talk with ‘him’ lasted about ten minutes. I spoke about how I had heard there was a bright white light. If he could just look around I was sure he could find it. I gave him a couple of seconds to look about. I was amazed at how I started to sense someone listening. I urged him to go towards the light and that I was sure an angel or two would be there to help if he let them. I am saying ‘he’ because I got a strong sense this spirit was male. By the time I was done, I felt he had moved on. The air in my room felt lighter. Our bedroom often had a dank smell that never came back after that day. All the noise and smoke alarm nonsense stopped as well. I was successful in moving a Spirit along and all it took was effort and sincerity on my part. I think most any of us could do this as well.

Bed and Breakfast

I had a bed and breakfast for a few years in my home that was haunted. A number of times I was asked to put the house on one of the busy tours that specialized in haunted bed and breakfasts. This is a hot item. I could not though, and would explain, much to the other innkeepers surprise, that it would be the equivalent of putting someone with a mental illness on display. It went against my humanity.

When we don't know where we are when we cross, we run the risk of hovering around as a ghost. When we are addicted *to anything*, including a home, we run the risk of being a ghost. A ghost is a spirit that has not moved on, has not grown, cannot or *will not* let go. They can stay in this state of stasis indefinitely. A home's remodel can stir them up and irritate them or any major disruption in their routine; a waking, sort of, from their murky reverie. Imagine drinking in an old established pub with your buddies and there layered in a different realm are the departed drinking alongside you. It happens, all the time. I have been asked by paranormal investigators to join forces with them. I politely decline from doing this as I am not interested in observing the dead. I find it remarkable that anyone would still doubt the dead exist and can be seen. I offer if they come across a client that wants to move the spirit along to a higher place, I will help. There are almost no takers on this. I have been told by paranormal investigators that the people that come to them do not want to lose their ghosts!

When I moved into my 1845 Greek Revival, I knew it came with company and lots of it. The house had been in the same family till we bought it. The first time I walked through the house after the closing, I could feel close to forty Spirits following me as I walked though each of the rooms! At one point, I stopped and said aloud that the home was ours now and that we would take very good care of it; and to please leave. Most left but there were a few hangers on. One very angry Spirit sent an antique glass vase flying across the room. I had placed the vase behind a TV, to keep it out of harm's way till we were through moving all the furniture. As I stood near my dresser that held the TV, I saw the vase lift vertically a few feet, then saw it veer to my left, shattering five feet away. I cried. It was my favorite material possession. It was an antique round green vase that was unusual because that shape almost never was retrievable from a bottle dig without the glass breaking. The color green was deep and gorgeous. I became enraged and told this Spirit he was out!

I assumed this was out of my league and sought the help of an established 'ghost buster'. I was directed to an old woman; her eyes completely white with cataracts, that I was told could do the trick. Her looks were exactly what one would expect a ghost buster to look like in my opinion. She channeled out a message from this disincarnate being in handwriting. She gave me the letter. He said his name was Robert and he claimed he was the caretaker of the house and we had no right to be there. She strongly suggested otherwise to him, reminding him the house was sold to us. The petite ghost buster ended up being effective in Robert's removal but it took a couple of tries. Not before he had sent my large black deacons bench, (that was nailed down on the front porch), flying one day before his final exit. He was mean and nasty.

Later, I asked the seller of the property if she had any idea who this 'Robert' fellow was. She looked me straight in the eye and said no. I did some digging at the local historical society and found out that this was her grandfather and he was the only one not buried at the family burial grounds a couple of miles down the road. He was a complete alcoholic that was kicked off the homestead. He went to live in western New York and at one point came back and stole his five year old daughter, dragging her while she kicked and cried for help, down the front staircase. Her mother got in a horse and buggy and found her daughter weeks later, and brought her safely home. This was before the advent of cars. I found this out because my neighbor *was* this little girl, now close to 100, and she remembered her horrific father vividly. This man was unhealthy when he was alive and he had not changed since his death.

This brings up a controversial topic, as was brought to my awareness the other night. A friend told me he had taken a course out in California by a famous psychic and the bottom line was, once everyone dies, they are fine...right? We have no pain, letting go of old attachments and wounds both physical and emotional.

I disagreed, firmly. He was shocked and reminded me that the person that taught this class is highly regarded. I have not seen this to be the case so I will go by my own experience and not take anothers' as the truth. It would be nice if we could be guaranteed a fluffy landing on the other side, and though much of the anguish of living is gone, there is no guarantee.

Let's put it this way: it is much better to have yourself in order now than hope to be removed of all personal responsibility just because you cross over to another realm. I have seen sadness, regret, apathy and more by some on the other side. Gratefully they seem to be in the minority, or maybe I don't 'see' these Spirits as much because they are not motivated to have a loving dialogue with my client.

Chapter Twelve

A Dark and Stormy Night

The moments that we have with friends and family, the chances that we have to make a big difference in the world or even to make a small difference to the ones we love, all those wonderful chances that life gives us, life also takes away. It can happen fast and a whole lot sooner than you think.
Larry Page, University of Michigan Commencement Address, 2009

While leading a small dreamwork class at my office in New Hampshire one evening, late in autumn, a sudden storm sprung outside; lightning, thunder and flash floods within two hours. But it was what happened during the drumming portion of the class that was more remarkable. A woman shared how she was having some dreams of her departed father. She also mentioned she was eating peanut butter crackers before she went to bed and was gaining weight. She told the group that her fathers' nighttime ritual was to have peanut butter crackers before he went to bed. My radar was up when I heard this. I am aware that the departed can inadvertently bring their energy so close to ours that we are susceptible to their addictions or just plain desires. It is worth checking ourselves if we develop habits that we did not previously have, as it could be an indicator that a departed person is sharing our energy field with us. I offered to see what I could in her dream, with her permission. I did not mention my concerns yet. She happily agreed.

We are able to travel in someone else's dream and glean information, that may be identical to what the dreamer saw or it may be a version that is similar. People new to Dreamwork, with no previous experience, can do this as well when taught how. As I started drumming, I immediately 'saw' my ex-husbands uncle, an accomplished Manhattan attorney. I was shocked. He happily and casually told me he had just passed and was thrilled he could connect with someone he knew. He asked me to contact some of the family and share his last thoughts and wishes and to make sure a favorite nephew got his collection of books. I agreed and was amazed.

Then I saw the father of the dreamer. He scolded me for trying to move him out of his daughter's energy field. He also told me that he and his wife were connected in a way I did not understand and it was none of my business poking into theirs. I was startled as I had never had a Spirit speak with me this way. I told him it was unhealthy and he was keeping his wife from moving on in her life. His daughter shared that her mother was still in a deep depression a year after his passing. He told me that his wife's depression would deepen if he pulled back and left any further. He told me to tell his daughter to suggest to her mother to take up swimming a couple of times a week to get out of the house. *"Tell her I will be there while she swims so she will not be alone."*

After the drumming I shared what I saw. The daughter confirmed that her mother never wanted to leave the house anymore. Additionally, her mother had recently said she might consider swimming but did not want to do it alone. I urged her to share what her father said to me.

I saw the dreamer months later and asked if her mother took up swimming. She told me that her mother was scared by what I saw, and did not take up swimming and was still quite depressed. This story might have a different ending if that same mother had known, prior to her husband's death and the grief it brought, that he would live on in a very real and active way. She might be more amendable to maintaining her relationship with him, even though it would be different.

Driving on my way home that night, I called my ex and told him I saw his uncle on the other side. He was unaware of what was happening with his uncle but called me back the next day and confirmed his dear uncle had just passed when I saw him. He told me his brother was happy to know that his uncle wanted him to have his books and also that he was still around, only in a new dimension.

Chapter Thirteen

Re- Incarnate

Everything you can imagine is real.
Pablo Picasso

I can't talk about Death and interdimensionality and not include some thoughts about reincarnation. Whether we believe in the linear march of time, a measured consistent, and predictable pace, (an idea becoming more and more outdated by science) or the generous shamanic understanding of it all happening simultaneously in the Now, we run into the concept of reincarnation. We can ignore all the cultures past and present who acknowledged this, and direct our attention on the humble daffodil for the secret of life.

Every Spring the demure daffodil shoots it green leaves up out of the cold ground, reaching, trusting that it will be received by the goodness of Sun and Rain, all of its needs being met and with no fear of being trampled on or destroyed. After stretching green arms up for a day or two, it sends forth the head of it's being; a lion-esque frill of yellow. It lives all the days of its life happily celebrating the Spring, only to die and return to the Earth from which it sprang just a short while back. The following year, without any prompting, it returns and starts the growing process anew. Does it remember doing this the previous year? Ask a daffodil.

This is what reincarnation feels like to me. I let go of my beloved body, take a needed rest in a nurturing place, and then come back for more. Maybe I come back to the Earth, maybe I go elsewhere. Maybe I alternate between all kinds of realities. This would make the most sense to me, since if I am a vast and Infinite Being, why would I choose only the Earth?

Derek Beres disbelieves in the possibility of reincarnation and says so, almost scathingly, yet puts forth: *The idea of rebirth is not new. Grave burials of Homo sapiens neanderthalensis date back to 200,000-75,000 B.C.E.; ritual tools suggest reentry after being "returned" to the original womb, the earth. Given that both hunting-gathering and agricultural societies (though, as Colin Tudge has suggested, they were one and the same before the advent of modern agriculture) relied on rebirth for grain and game, it makes sense that our forebears would believe our souls did the same. We plant a seed, it grows, flowers, dies, and the soil again rebirths sustenance during the next cycle.*

Joseph Campbell thought our original "birth trauma" - the moment we exit the womb before our lungs begin to work, which results in an intense grasping of air that can cause dizziness and blackout - served as a fitting analogy for what we encounter whenever suffering trauma. Every "threshold passage" we walk through is another metaphorical exit from the womb, which gave rise not only to the idea of being born again in this lifetime, but from lifetime to lifetime as well.

I had a waking dream of a life in Egypt. (for more information on a waking dream see my book***; The Power of Dreams: Dream Tools for Navigating Your Life***) I have had five dreams of different lives in Egypt. One life I remember is around the mid 1200's BC and I am dancing in a sacred trancelike state, in a large room with other dancers. (My movements resemble belly dancing, only I am aware there is meaning of each swing of my hips or sway of my arms) I look down and see what I am wearing. I notice arm bracelets that are silver bands on my wrists and at my elbows. They are joined together by five thin braids of silver. I love to dance and offer my dance as a prayer to God. Each movement is a physical blessing and prayer to both the Divine and the Earth. My husband (if that is what he would be called) is shared by many women and he is also the pharaoh. I am his favorite most of the time. I have a ten year old son by him who is in a small room nearby the room that I am dancing in. I am aware that after a certain amount of dancing I would 'fall' onto the floor, spent. My pharaoh sits on a small throne- like chair watching all of us dance. I know he is joyous but his emotions are difficult to read by his expression.

Suddenly, there erupts into our space a chaos of men and noise and clashing and yelling. I stand shocked and stunned, unable to comprehend what is happening in that immediate moment. They grab the pharaoh and drag him out of the room. They grab us, and as they do, our beautiful dancing turns into screams and bodies twisting to get away. There is swift violence. While some men are grabbing us, other men are breaking the sacred objects in our temple room. They are yelling in a language I do not know. My life skips to a point, weeks later, and I am back in the temple room, only now all sacred objects are gone. Some of the women dancers are there, but many are missing. My pharaoh is gone and in his seat is a foreign man whom I detest with every cell of my being. He has a crude smile and is mocking us to dance for him. His desire is for sexual entertainment and has nothing to do with the sacred. He is aware that I dance in a trance fashion and he very much wants me to do this. I refuse, knowing it will bring about my death. I am also aware of my son, who is still alive. I make the choice to live, primarily for my son, and dance, but do not show them my sacred dance. I never dance honoring the Divine again in that life and die at the young age of twenty seven from a broken spirit, just a few years after the invasion.

I wake from this dream excited knowing that the intensity of the experience pointed to the strong possibility of a past life; at least certainly something worth exploring. This is one of those times that I am grateful for my lack of any formal education past high school. (I spent the last three years of high school in the art room painting; for all intents purposes, my western academic education stopped in ninth grade. I loved school until the ninth grade, but loved painting more, and chose the latter and the school acquiesced because they were more interested in my graduating than dropping out, which I informed them I would do if I had to endure another long day at a desk. This was in the late seventies and maybe it was easier then to be ‘out of the box’. I was not only thinking ‘out of the box’; I was living ‘out of the box’. After painting most of the morning, I would leave school each day at 1:00 and hike in the nearby woods for an hour, and then work at my job waitressing till 10:00 or 11:00 at night. I was self-determined! My father left parenting decisions to my mother regarding their daughters. My mother was part Native American and though she was very firm and tougher than most of my friends mothers in some areas, she also said the most important thing she could do as a mother was 'not break our Spirit.' She called me her Lion Daughter, primarily because of my long, wild hair but maybe because of my wild nature too.

Back to my education or lack thereof; I knew I had not had this dream because of some memory of something I had read on Egypt. I had never studied anything at all about Egypt, so this made me all the more curious. This waking dreaming was before the internet or google; I went to a bookstore and bought a book on ancient Egypt and found invasions in the time period of my waking dream. Around 1279 BC, Ramesses II, also known as Ramesses the Great, ascended the throne, and went on to build more temples, erect more statues and obelisks, and sire more children than any other pharaoh in history. A bold military leader, Ramesses II led his army against the Hittites in the Battle of Kadesh and, after fighting to a stalemate, finally agreed to the first recorded peace treaty, circa 1258 BC. Egypt withdrew from much of the Near East after this, leaving the Hittites to compete unsuccessfully with the growing power of a resurgent Assyria and the newly arrived Phrygians.

In the end the rise of another power, Assyria, convinced both Ramesses and Hattusili II of Hatti to come to terms, and in c. 1259 BC they agreed to divide Syria between them. There is also mention in the records of problems in the harem and speculation one of the women plotted to make her son the next pharaoh, though he was not next in line.

I met an Egyptian woman a few years later that taught belly dancing. I told her my 'dream' and showed her some of the dance moves I remembered. Her expression dropped and she urged me to show her husband who reacted the same way. They told me there are hand and arm movements not normally taught in most belly dancing classes, and that I was executing them flawlessly.

Suicide Sam

Sam was not a man but an elephant. I was seven and on a field trip to the Springfield Museum of Science in Massachusetts with my fellow second graders. This was our first field trip and our teacher went to great lengths to make sure we understood what was expected of us; mainly stay together and keep your hands to yourself. I was the most obedient of children so this posed no problem; that is till I met Sam.

The rest of the day is a blur, except when my class turned the corner into a small room in the museum, filled in all directions with an elephant. I gasped. We slowly walked the narrow space around him, my eyes never leaving this mammoth beast. The teacher briskly read the plaque that had information about Suicide Sam and then continued onto the exhibit in the next room; the children following her like baby ducks. I did not.

I was overwhelmed with emotion and could not leave this elephant. Instead I sat next to him and touched him. I knew he was not alive and that he was a stuffed version of his former self. I also knew I loved him with all my seven year old heart. My teacher found me ten minutes later and was horrified to see, my eyes swollen red with tears, me holding onto a dead elephant. She whisked me over to the others and later called my mother. My mother was incredulous that I would get into any trouble let alone hiding out with a dead elephant crying.

What none of us knew then, and I came to know later, was a life I had many centuries back, in which I was the caretaker of an elephant. I was a boy in India and it was my job to take care of a sacred pachyderm who was my constant companion 24/7, till I was in my mid- twenties. When he died, my heart broke and I was unable to take care of another elephant after that for reasons I do not remember. I think I just never had the opportunity again. I adored that elephant; and Suicide Sam grabbed at my Soul in a way my mind could not understand.

One of the most moving displays of elephant emotion is the grieving process. Elephants remember and mourn loved ones, even many years after their death. When an elephant walks past a place that a loved one died he or she will stop and take a silent pause that can last several minutes. While standing over the remains, the elephant may touch the bones of the dead elephant (not the bones of any other species), smelling them, turning them over and caressing the bones with their trunk. ~Nature/ PBS

I loved that elephant, in the way that an elephant loves.

Chapter Fourteen

Tarot and Black Dogs

A door is what a dog is perpetually on the wrong side of.
Ogden Nash

I read Tarot, primarily for myself. It gives me a 'sounding board' of sorts confirming my intuition. There is one card I dread and have often thought of just removing from my deck altogether and that is (and for people familiar with Tarot they already know what I am going to say); The Tower. Even thinking of it sends chills down my spine.

There is a Death Card in the Tarot which does little to disturb my peace of mind, unlike The Tower. In the well- known Rider Waite Tarot deck the Death card looks like you might expect; a skeleton atop a horse (white!) looking rather friendly to me. He is bearing a flag with a rosette pattern and the card is understood to mean death; death of a person or death of a situation. When I see this card I think of transformation and change, which is palatable for me.

The Tower card features a tower with two people falling from it, flames roaring out the windows of the medieval looking stone edifice.

Dark and gloomy clouds are looming as well as lightning striking the tower. This is the card of utter destruction, and this is why I fear it. It is a card of hopelessness to me as well. I still may take it out of my deck, but maybe it is better that I keep it as a reminder that as long as I never pull it, there is hope in most any situation.

I bring this up because it is another touchstone in my life that connects me to my mortal humanity and death; another reminder that even as I read tarot cards (almost daily) I have a subtle dance with Death. It is in the deck.

Ancient Egypt

Along this same line, the ancient Egyptians called the Guardian to the Gates of the Underworld Anubis. You will recognize him as the black headed jackal with the body of a man.

"Anubis was associated with the mummification and protection of the dead for their journey into the afterlife. He was usually portrayed as a half human, half jackal, or in full jackal form wearing a ribbon and holding a flail in the crook of its arm. The jackal was strongly associated with cemeteries in ancient Egypt, since it was a scavenger which threatened to uncover human bodies and eat

their flesh. The distinctive black color of Anubis "did not have to do with the jackal (per se) but with the color of rotting flesh and with the black soil of the Nile valley, symbolizing rebirth.

Anubis is depicted in funerary contexts where he is shown attending to the mummies of the deceased or sitting atop a tomb protecting it. In fact, during embalming, the "head embalmer" wore an Anubis costume. The critical weighing of the heart scene in the ***Book of the Dead*** *also shows Anubis performing the measurement that determined the worthiness of the deceased to enter the realm of the dead ……" Wikipedia*

This reminds me that we paint make up on our deceased, in an effort to make them look more alive than dead. I am more disturbed by the obvious spackling on of cream colored makeup than the white/gray pallor of death. I want to take a warm facecloth to the dead. I do not want any such stuff on me, I want to look as dead as I am. This is interesting to me since I have worn make up every day of my life since I was about fourteen, yet in Death I will take a break!

Black Dogs

I find comfort in this dog- like Being and associate black dogs as harbingers of luck and protection because of Anubis. I have had many black dogs as pets and they are invariably awesome guardians. Years ago, I had a beautiful wrought iron bench stolen from my yard on New Years' Eve. I was upset as this was also the bench for my young kids to sit on while waiting for their school bus. I sent out an urgent prayer to God requesting a black dog! My argument was that if I had a black dog this would never have happened! I also added to the request that the dog be free since money was tight. Two weeks later someone was looking for a good home for their black dog and asked us if we would like him. What luck! He was an enormous black Lab and Newfoundland mix named Rembrandt, he was very loving, and yet meant business also. It is not that bad things can't happen around a black dog, it's just that, I believe, the odds are in favor of the good if there is a black dog present. Once Rembrandt pulled a column off our front porch trying to catch up with me as I went to get the mail, he did not flinch as he dragged the ten foot column behind him. Years later, when Rembrandt died, I wailed.

November is the month of death for me, black the color, pomegranates the food, violin the instrument, gray birch in winter its' tree, and the direction West. This personal method of understanding is understood by poets, shamans and children. I hope the instrumental rendition of *The Texas Waltz*, performed by David

Bromberg, is played at my funeral; it reminds

me of the ups and downs of a well lived life.

2008~ In their efforts to preserve Abenkai ways and traditions, the Koasek Abenaki tribe recently accepted the return of their ancestral corn seeds. The corn, which has been out of Abenaki hands for more than three centuries, was given to them by Charlie and Sarah Calley.

Part Two

Chapter Fifteen

The Departed Have Something to Say

Doubt is not a pleasant condition, but certainty is absurd.
Voltaire

"Oh...I hope I can remember this!" These are words I say at many of my readings that I do as a psychic Medium. I am able to connect easily with the departed yet I retain very little of what I see, even minutes after a reading. This is a blessing because I have enough just living my own life, and would not find it beneficial

retaining the memories of so many people that I also read for. But I do come across some very insightful Souls on the other side, and from time to time, I wish I could have a verbatim record of what has been said.

My fluency in speaking with other realms has not always been so. But as you can see with the stories from previous chapters, it is my natural inclination. There are many, many stories actually but I chose the ones that had a flavor of their own, so we can have a more rounded conversation about death.

I was tricked into reading as a psychic. I was tricked by Ramona Garcia and the Universe. Ramona is a self- proclaimed, world renowned psychic who looks nothing like her name. She is petite, blondish and of a certain age that would amount to a lot of centuries. She wears copious amounts of jewelry, big and colorful and bulky and not proportional to her size at all; just like my own grandmother did. People love her and I did instantly as well. Small but mighty she is. At a fundraiser a couple of years back, she marched (in a somewhat hobbled manner) toward me yelling as loud as her soft voice could get, "What are you doing sitting there like that?"

My response, *"I am waiting for a dream. Do you have one?"*

"Stop this.....you are a reader! You are psychic and need to read now because we have two lines of people waiting to be read at this event and we will be here all night at this rate!"

"I am sorry but I am not a psychic nor do I read."

"I am the internationally famous Ramona Garcia of Salem and I know what I am talking about! she bellowed. "You are a psychic if there ever was one, so start reading…*now*!" She reached me and grabbed my hands looking carefully at my palms and double jointed thumbs. She turned and as she walked away she yelled over her shoulder to the woman calling out for the next person to be read in line; "Tell them Susan is a Reader and psychometrist!" With that announced, I had someone sitting at my table in two seconds and every fifteen minutes from then on that evening.

I was unsure of what a psychometrist was. I vaguely recalled a class I had taken many years back with a very gifted Medium Elaine Kuzmeskus, who had each of the participants place a small personal object on an antique silver tray that was passed around the room. She then had us close our eyes, and as she re-passed the tray, each of us took an item from it. With eyes still closed, we held the object trying to sense the story and/or the owner of the objects energy connected to it. It was remarkable how easy this was for most everyone there. This is psychometry.

But now I have a person in front of me, who when I asked if she had anything she would like me to hold and read, replies no. Out of desperation and not knowing what else to do, I ask to hold her hand. I close my eyes and say a quick prayer softly aloud,

"We come here today seeking guidance and healing for _________. May only that which is good and true and for ____________ highest good come through today. May I have clear and unobstructed guidance from my Guardians and Guides. May I also have the help of ___________________Guardians and Guides."

And then, as if watching a screen with sight not associated with my normal waking reality, I saw people and heard stories. I was amazed. I was also amazingly accurate, much to my own surprise. Since I have no idea why I can do this, I also have no idea how long it will last. I did not qualify nor train for this skill. It works like turning on a switch. When I am done with the reading, I thank my Guides for their help as well as the Guides of the person I read for. I open my eyes and that turns the switch back off.

I went home that night, tired and none too happy with my new skill. My heart is entirely focused on teaching others how to navigate by their own intuition and especially their dreams. How can I be reconciled with this? My daughter told me that night, "Who cares? You are a single mom with bills to be paid. Be glad you can do this!" She was right about the bills. On any given day there are more of them than the resources to pay them. My plan was to do this once a month, and that's all. But it has taken on a life of its own and I now read for people all the time. I still struggle with the ethics of this sometimes. I really want to empower people *to rely on their own natural intuition*, but along with teaching people how to work with their dreams and also how to read from the Oracle that speaks around us all the time, I read as a Medium. So many people have told me that the peace and confirmation of hearing from the other side has made a very big difference in their life, so I find comfort in this. It also has occurred to me that I would not be given this gift if it was not meant for me to share it. Within a month, my readings took a decided turn towards speaking with the departed.

And they have a lot to say! Most of the departed are very grateful to have someone in this realm hear them so they can have a dialogue with us. I am the operator of a three way conversation. I hear the departed and I repeat verbatim what they say, and then let the person I am reading for respond. Usually the departed can hear them, but if, for some reason, they cannot hear what was just said on this side, then I repeat, verbatim, what the client just said. This goes back and forth anywhere from fifteen to thirty minutes. I do not like to do it any longer than that for one person. It takes all my focus to propel and maintain an aspect of myself to what feels like a midway point between them and us. The person on the other side has to do the same, and hold their energy at a certain vibration for clear communication to continue. This is a mutual effort and very demanding on me physically, though I am sitting with my eyes closed. My body does not want to be so close to the land of the dead perhaps. My Spirit is fluid, but my body rebels. On days when I do this for many hours, I am completely spent the next day. I don't answer my phone or emails and spend the day doing simple physical tasks like painting my barn, mowing the grass, gardening and the like. I reground myself to this world in a conscious way. I could not do readings every day, all day long. One time, after a long night of readings at a private home, midnight came and there were still two more people to read. I informed my host I had to stop. I was done. She became very mad and reminded me these two people had been waiting. (I must say on my own behalf that more people came than had originally been scheduled. I can only do so many readings in a row) I tried to explain that I was spent and so fuzzy I could barely remember my name! I left and was not surprised I did not hear back from her. It occurred to me that it would be helpful for me to explain what is required of me to do a reading of this nature, so that expectations could be met. This is not like card reading, which is not physically demanding at all for me.

Some days I am cavalier about this skill and say tongue in cheek; I talk to the dead people. Sometimes after back to back readings, I can't stand to hear any more talking from either side. Everyone be quiet! There is the added demand on my concentration that the people on *this* side are looking for as much information and conversation as they can squeeze in a reading and the other side is pretty much the same…..urgently conveying emotional communication, as quickly as they can, before the ‘door’ closes. I do not facilitate a natural conversation between two people, but an intense, emotional exchange (most of the time) with the shift of my consciousness.

I do not mean to be complaining. Rather, I would like to see an increased awareness of the process required for any of us to speak with people that have dropped their bodies.

Here are some things I now know from my experience:

1) Initially, we go exactly where we think we will when we cross.

2) There is a place that could be associated with the term purgatory. A place better described as soft gray and it neither here nor there.

3) Sudden death can put us in a state of shock for a 'time' over there. Angels

watch closely in these situations, yet let us ‘wake up’ at our own pace.

4)

Our personalities don’t change much.

5)

We are outside time and space and heartache only can happen in a time/space dimension.

6)

We can call them to us.

7)

We don't want to call them to us.

8)

We are the judge of our own deeds. God is greater than judge. We are harsher on ourselves than God would be.

9)

There are an infinite amount of levels and places to go to.

10)

We don't want to hang out nonstop with our relatives over there. We don't want to do it here and we don't want to do it there either.

11)

Generally, many men like to do projects they were unable to do here due to time constraints and responsibilities. They like to be alone often too.

12)

Most women like to cluster over there just like over here. They are more social.

13)

I have had many recipes given to share from the other side. Favorite recipes while they were alive.

14)

The more open and adventurous the personality, the easier they can be heard.

15)

Pets, especially dogs, hang out with us over there.

16)

There are places similar to our hospitals. Angels work there.

17)

Due to our problems when we cross, we can feel lost over there.

18)

Prayers from this side absolutely help them on the other side. Especially newbies that have crossed.

19)

Sometimes babies and children that have crossed continue to grow up, but usually they present themselves at about the same age, and are very aware of what family they are connected to.

20)

They cannot influence our lives, even if they wanted to.

21)

Heaven can be also described as the astral realm.

22)
There are dual states, of every imaginable combination, as life on Earth is a dual state.

23)
There are 'higher' non dual states we can go to.

24)
Most Souls do not go to a non-dual state, but stick with the familiar dual state of existence. Then reincarnate.

25)
The very spiritually inclined spend 'time' in realms with like-minded Souls.

26)

Most everyone wants forgiveness and understanding.

27)

They do visit in dreams, and send messages in their unique ways; songs on radio, butterflies, white feathers, pennies etc.

28)

Any time I ask for a' host of heavenly angels' for help for someone on the other side, I only get three. Three effective angels.

29)

If someone would have thought it bad to talk with a psychic when they were alive, they will probably feel the same over there.

30)
Most of us stay close to the Earth when we first cross.

31)
They do not like to see us broken hearted for them.

32)
They paint and sing and dance and travel and cook and fish and boat and all manner of fun!

33)
There is no sickness or pain. Ever.

34)
They are at peace when they have not left loose ends.

35)

Some, especially people that were devoted parents, still want to offer help.

36)

The most dominating or loving personalities are at the gate of death welcoming us when we die.

37)

We have complete choice of who we want to spend ‘time’ with over there, but this is a mutual choice. There is an energetic buffer between people that are best not together.

38)

Many are surprised they can speak with us here.

39)

They can cry tears of joy.

40)

They can hug and kiss us though we don't see or feel it.

41)

Our relationships can still grow, even improve, regardless of the veil.

42)

Moms still feel like Moms. (usually)

43)

We do not want to over mourn our dead.

44)

I have not seen Hell.

45)

I am not afraid to die.

46)

Love never stops. How do I know? Love is not locked in the time/space continuum, it is not temporal. The truth is not temporal.

Chapter Sixteen

We Are Choosers

We shall not cease from exploration. And the end of all our exploring will be to arrive where we started and know the place for the first time.
T. S. Eliot

This is important to ponder and understand. It is the primary reason for my desire to write this book. It could be summed up in one sentence: "*We go where we think we will go.*" We go *exactly* where we think we will go when we cross. At least this is the case initially.

In the case of the angry spirit Robert mentioned in an earlier chapter, he stayed on at the home that was denied him in life. The wound from his forced exile must have been very deep, he could not move on. My guess too is that there was no one praying and interceding for him when he crossed, which added to his inability to go to a better place. Not only did his family (justifiably) kick him out of the house, (at least three families were living under that roof, all brothers with their wives and children), they sent his body to a grave in the opposite direction from where all his ancestors had been buried since they landed on this continent in the 1700's. Roberts' anger was seething and he was all too happy to unleash it on me.

In my same home at that time was another gentler spirit, a girl of about ten, who was seen by many of us. She would open the dining room door for me sometimes if my hands were full. The door knob would turn and the door open. I found out with some more digging, that this was the niece that had died and spent most of her time at the house, even living there during the summers. I prayed for her to move on, to be with her mother, and 'saw' a joyous reunion happen.

I would like to see all of us treat our departed this way. We have the ability to ensure safe passage. Certainly, our ancestors knew the importance of prayer for the newly departed, so that they would make a safe and thorough crossing. Somehow, down the line, we have been fed the lies that only a priest can do this. I argue that any of us can do this and be effective, if it is done in love and with the requested blessing of God. We will only be compelled to help the departed, if we know in our hearts, that we do in fact carry on. There is a difference between hoping we carry on, hedging our bets that we carry on; and a deep knowing that we will always carry on.

There was never a 'time' when we were not, and there will never come a 'time' when we are not. Nothing new has come into existence and nothing is leaving. There is only a change of expression.

Sometimes when my kids were little I would remind them that dinosaur pee was still on the Earth. It could not leave and disappear. It went into the rain clouds, came back down and maybe it was in their drinking water, only clean now. They would have a fit hearing they might be drinking dinosaur urine. The flip side is that all the water that the holiest have drunk is also still here. All the snow since the beginning of time is here. Air breathed by the best artists of antiquity still circulates. I think it is good to experience mental conundrums. It helps us think outside of the box. We have boxed ourselves, to our own demise, into believing all the magic of life is gone and we have a reason and answer for everything. That is except death, it is the one thing that we are not permitted to place in a small container of understanding.

When we can expand our awareness of ourselves we can gain a better understanding of death. When we can know that we exist simultaneously, in other dimensions across time and space, then death takes on a whole new role. Its pallor grows rosy. *Please let there be breaks of distinction in my Being that only death can bring*. I can multiply myself when I have death offering me closure of one aspect. My Being can become a kaleidoscope of my Self, each beautiful aspect delineated by death. Death adds beauty to my Being when seen this way. Creation and Destruction can only go hand in hand; one cannot exist without the other. It is this duality that is spoken about across cultures, and the only third option is when we rise out of all duality and exist as a Godhead, which is also 'always' happening. A triangle of Being, the holy trinity. 'Always' is captioned, since this aspect of ourselves, exists outside time and space, so the concept 'always' does not apply in a literal way, but it is hard finding words to describe a nonlinear concept.

Let's try a quick way to understand a few aspects of ourselves: One aspect is the part of you reading this now. Another part is aware of your immediate environment. (I am assuming this last one since only an advanced yogic type could put 100 percent of their attention on the immediate now.) One part is the steady maintenance aspect of your body, the part that is easily understood if you think about how you maintain all your organs etc. while sleeping. There is also all the parts that have lived up till now. No part of your life has entirely disappeared, and a strong intuitive person can tap into your old story with just a little effort and see your two year old self, ten year old self, twenty year old self and all the in-betweens.

There are your past lives that also still exist in some un-nameable realm that can be accessed for proof if need be. Here are five layers that most people would agree exist. Let's add lives that coulda, shoulda been led, if you had made different choices at key forks in the roads of your life. These are recognized in the world of quantum physics so let's include them here. It is easy to see a myriad of aspects of one person without delving too deeply. We are very much like a sun with the rays being aspects of our Being extending out in all directions. That is a good analogy that comes close to whom we actually are; immense, never ending Beings of Light and Creation.

Now, tell me why anyone would be fascinated to think that a house may be haunted? It is a 'low rent' understanding of what a Human Being truly is. It is a flat understanding of reality.

One big benefit of 'old time religion' is that we had a belief system that told us where we all would go after death. If we were good, we were met at the pearly gates of heaven by St. Peter and perhaps a few loving relatives. We all then rested forever in peace. If we were bad, we burned in hell for all eternity, crying in painful anguish; forever. Forever is too long a concept for most of us to wrap our minds around. It is certainly too much for me. A God that would punish anyone, in a tortuous way forever, is also too much for my mind (and heart) to wrap around. Every time I think God would judge anyone that harshly, my mind can't help but drift to the sun that comes up every day, for all of us, whether we deserve it or not. I am reminded of the stars and flowers as well. Can the same Creator that created this paradise also be one that would place any of us in writhing pain forever?

I was in California, hiking my way up the coast (paradise if there ever was), when I heard over the news that a man in Norway killed 77 people in a bomb attack and gun rampage committing acts of terror in Oslo and on Utoya Island in July of 2011.

I was shocked. Who would do this, and certainly not such a clean cut looking fellow! His outside appearance did not reflect his profound sickness inside. Almost immediately I thought, what on Earth should we do with people like this? My heart broke when I heard of the children killed in the 2012 Newtown, Connecticut shootings as well.

I am not a proponent of the death penalty. Not for any reason other than I think it just delays the problem, which is sickness of the Soul. I see us go from life to life, in a reincarnated way, so what possible good can come from killing someone if their Soul is messed up, only to have it come back; maybe worse than ever! I have an idea; instead of killing killers and rapists and all manner of bad people; we incarcerate them; and bring in the holiest of us alive on Earth, to go sit with them; perhaps saying nothing, no dialogue. This is not about talking sense into them, nor talking them into Soul health. Soul health does not come about by linear methods, including speech. It comes about by heart centered Being. How about if the Dali Lama sat in for a few hours? He could even just sit and read a book quietly to himself. His vibration would be so high that a metamorphosis would start to result. We could ask the top fifty of us alive today to dedicate a part of their lives to this; a weekly visit to the worst of the worst of us. We need the best of the best to be with the worst of the worst. We know that when we are in the presence of a high level human being we are uplifted. It may take year upon year of weekly visits to affect a change, but it would be worth it, since the result would be a Soul in an active state of healing, refining and redefining itself. This solution speaks directly to the statement by Einstein, "*You cannot solve a problem from the same consciousness that created it. You must learn to see the world anew.*" We need to think outside our usual box, and my guess is that the simpler the better. This technique is simple and we have nothing to lose. They would be incarcerated either way, only instead of surrounding with more of what they are, we surround them with the blazing light of goodness; conversion by vibration. We are nothing more than vibration, validated by quantum physicists:

"*We know from quantum physics that everything in the entire universe is pure energy. The difference is in the unique vibration everything has inherent to itself. Quantum physics also accepts that energy is influenced by energy and like energy attracts in accordance with its true vibration. This is how the law of Attraction works throughout the universe. That which is in vibrational harmony will be attracted to each other.*

A pair of tuning forks can demonstrate an example of this. If one tuning fork, placed at a distance from another tuning fork is struck thereby emitting a certain vibration, it will in fact cause the other tuning fork to vibrate at the exact same frequency. This is a very simple example of how like energy with the same vibrational frequencies are attracted to each other" ~ Kevin Forrester.

We cannot help but have our vibratory field adjusted for bad or good; so let's choose the brighter of the two.

The soft gray of Purgatory

Often I can see how a person has passed. If they have crossed in a sudden accident, they may or may not realize they are dead. They may still be in a state of shock and neither here nor there in their awareness. This is nothing to be too alarmed about though, because from what I can see, we are never left completely on our own, but are always watched over and cared for by Angelic Beings. They do not normally rush us along though either. When I see this, I ask for help to bring awareness to that person about the fact that they have crossed over and to keep them moving along to a better state of existence. I have seen some literally blink their eyes and look around as if wakened from a deep sleep.

A primary funeral ritual, across all cultures, was to pray the dead along, for a safe crossing; no stopping for the Soul till they reached their ultimate destination; please don't hover in the gray Nether World but continue on till you reach the point where there is light and love. When we pray for a loved one that has recently crossed, I think it is better to focus on assuring them we will be okay and they just need to get to where they are going. Holding them too close to us through our grief, may keep them from making a complete crossing. In life, good parents know that sometimes the best they can do for their children is to let them go and grow; assuring them that regardless they will always have their parents love. This is a healthy approach for our departed as well.

Bigger than death is Love, and we will always be connected through the strongest bond in the Universe; Love.

Chapter Seventeen

WE CAN CALL THEM TO US.
WE DON'T WANT TO CALL THEM TO US.

Let this be our prayer when we lose our way,
Lead us to a place, guide us with your grace,
to a place where we'll be safe.
Andrea Bocelli

I was reading for a woman who had lost her best friend. She came to me hoping I would be able to reach him. I did. I also saw her profound grief was keeping him from creating his life over there. I told her I saw this and her reply (to my utter shock) was, "I know this. I speak to him throughout the day and even tell him he cannot leave me yet." No matter how much I tried to explain to her that her behavior was selfish, her reply was always the same; "I need him too much to let him go yet." She left and on her way toward the door, she yelled back to me, " Maybe in a few months I will let him go." I was horrified.

During another reading a woman called me numerous times before a private reading event to ask if I was the 'real deal' and if I could authentically connect with the departed. I was red flagged by her intensity but read for her a week later at the event regardless. Within a couple of minutes it became clear why she wanted me to help her. I immediately connected with her deceased father who appeared very loving and apologized for things he did and didn’t do while alive. His daughter quickly went into a small fury about all sorts of small things and then her anger picked up when she was left nothing in his will. All his humble Earthly belongings went to his devoted wife, her step mom. This was the rub for her and she lamb blasted him for about fifteen minutes over it. I was horrified. She apologized. As she left, but I made a mental note to never read for her again, nor will I let a reading continue if the primary goal is to continue an argument from both sides of the veil. I will never be the ‘medium’ for that to happen again.

If during a reading a person has not come through that the client wants to connect with, I ask politely if I can speak with so and so. I then hear the person's name called out by a Spirit I cannot see, and most often they then come through. It seems as though their awareness was not in the direction of this realm and that is why they did not come through originally.

Occasionally I am blocked from connecting with an individual and usually I am shown why; they are not ready to stretch their awareness to two realms.

Chapter Eighteen

Our Personalities Don't Change Much

We did not change as we grew older; we just became more clearly ourselves.
Lynne Hall

I have found that most often the first people to 'come through' are the people that had a more extroverted personality while alive; at least they are the easiest to hear. Also, mothers seem to come through quicker than fathers; and this is perhaps because they are usually the ones more intimately connected to our everyday lives and routines. The nuances of our lives are still interesting to them. One mother came through (though she had been deceased for over ten years) to give very practical advice on encouraging a vacation on the Cape. She went on further to say that if five days felt like too much time off, how about three. It was important! After the reading the grown daughter of this woman confirmed everything and made sure to take a few days off to go to the Cape, though she had been wavering previous to the reading.

Almost a dozen times I have had grandmothers and mothers share their favorite recipe, some of them sound delicious! More of these came from Italians than non-Italians.

If we are not too keen about the morality of speaking with the dead, we will not be too inclined to communicate when we pass. One woman who came through held a white cross out in front of her as she approached me, but she did communicate at least.

Sometimes the departed will ask who I am and what am I doing. I answer quickly and bring the focus back to the person sitting in front of me. This reminds me that we do not become ‘all seeing and knowing’ after we cross,

otherwise they would not ask these types of

questions.

Chapter Nineteen

I Have Not Seen Hell

Hope is a waking dream.
Aristotle

If Hell exists I have not seen it; at least not in the classic way of a devil in a landscape of fire and brimstone. I *have* seen Hell on Earth. When we are disconnected from our awareness of the sacred, we open the door for all manner of everything hurtful. Since we are all interwoven, we are also subjected to horror via another, as it can and does affect us all.

One thing I like to remind myself (although it is emotionally removed), is that as long as we live in creation, we are subjected to duality; the good, bad and indifferent. I can consciously bring my awareness into a non-duality state of being while alive and also when I pass if I choose. Currently, I am only able to do this in small batches of 'time'. I parenthesize time as we enter a non-time state of being in the non-dual state. Miracles happen more easily in the non-dual state, since we are free of the hindrances that only exist in the dual state.

Chapter Twenty

We Do Not Want To Over Mourn Our Dead

The worst thing of all is standing by when folks are doing something wrong.
Kirby Larson, Hattie Big Sky, 2006

I was asked many years ago to meet with a family who had recently lost their teenage son in a murder. I did not want to go and, furthermore, did not know at that time how I *could* help. But, I was asked by a friend, so I agreed to go. I got lost finding the home and when I arrived I felt self-conscious as I squeezed my oversized, (obnoxiously so),

SUV into a small driveway filled with cars in various states of disrepair. As if this was not enough conspicuousness, I also had in large, bold white letters: “got dreams?” across the back window. I carried my drum bag up the staircase of the apartment building; loud voices and music coming from all the apartments. I was nervous and afraid my car, or I, would be robbed.

I knocked on the door of one of the apartments and a young, pleasant looking Spanish woman opened it and gave me a big smile. She waved me into her tiny home and suggested I sit at the kitchen table that was five feet in from the door. As I sat I noticed that an older Spanish woman was standing in the corner glaring at me, the antithesis of the welcome I just received from her daughter. I came to know that the mother understood English but spoke only Spanish and the daughter was fluent in both languages. I started off by acknowledging I did not know how I could help but that our mutual friend sent me. I asked permission to set up a candle I had in my bag, along with a few other special things including sage, on the table in front of me. This eased the tension a bit. The daughter told me that her brother had been shot a couple of months prior and the grief was overwhelming for her mother still. The mother stood frowning at me, never diverting her gaze for a moment.

I said a prayer aloud, closed my eyes and softly beat my frame drum. Immediately I saw her departed son in the corner of the kitchen, behind his mother. I tell the mother and sister that I can see him and describe what he looks like. They confirm my description. I now know I have the right person. (an important step!) He tells them (through me) that he is in that corner of the kitchen always. I ask incredulously, why? His response is that he took care of his family while he was alive and they still need him. He tells me he did *everything*; cooking, shopping, managing the household on all fronts. They confirm this, or rather the daughter confirms this and the mother continues to look at me cynically.

I gently tell him that he can know that his mother and sister will be alright and they can now learn how to take care of themselves. It would be much healthier for him to move along toward a higher dimension, and he can always come back to quickly check in. He tells me he would like to but he cannot leave, plus he loved food and the kitchen. His mother starts to quietly weep. I see the mother and son are entwined energetically and the daughter is ready to throw her hands in the air. After a lot of effort I am able to get him to agree to move on, even if for only small bursts. He tells them (through me) that he wants his mother to give all his clothes to his friends and stop hoarding them in his room. She shakes her head emphatically this is not so. The daughter gives her mom a sharp glance. He also wants his mother to know he deeply loved his girlfriend and she was a 'good girl' even though the mother never liked her. The mother scoffs at this. He wants his mother to give his girlfriend the picture of the both of them. The mother shakes her head vehemently no, and says (through the daughter) that there was no photo. He gets mad and says, "Yes there is! It is in the nice wooden frame and you have even started trying to pry the photo out!" The mother freezes and the daughter's eyes go wide at this comment. She jumps up and runs to his room. I notice the piles of his clothes everywhere in his old room. His sister comes back with the photo of him and his girlfriend. It is wooden and we can see where 'someone' started to remove the photo.

I now have the attention of all three and the bullshit stops. The mother drops her head and cries. She agrees to his 'demands' which include giving the photo to his girlfriend and telling her that he loved her deeply (and he said so in the reading), that she give away his clothes to his friends, that she make peace with the mother of the young man who shot him (they had been friends for more years than enemies) reminding her that, in a way, she also lost her son since he would be incarcerated for many, many years, and finally, that she go visit his grave. (his mother had not been yet)

I heard months later that the mother and sister were doing much better and the mother had done everything she promised her son that day.

Recently, I learned his mother was in a program that helped others deal with grief from similar situations. I am quite sure her son is proud of her and how she was able to endure her intense heartache, find her way through it and even help others! She learned not to over mourn her son and because of that *he* was able to build a new life in heaven and she learned how to build a new life here.

Chapter Twenty One

A Gift of Life

Life shrinks or expands in proportion to one's courage.
Anais Nin

I was irritated and grumpy as I pulled into my driveway after a long day; the cold and pouring rain adding to my gloom. While still in my car, I get a call asking me to show someone from Craigslist two chairs for sale in my barn. I agree begrudgingly. Fifteen minutes later a dark haired, robust woman pulls up. She walks determinedly to my barn and agrees to buy the two chairs. When I offer to help her load them into her vehicle, she declines the offer saying she works with men all day and hauls stuff all the time. I watch her as she tosses them into place. Amusement is replacing my gloom.

She plunks herself down on a couch, (also for sale in my barn), introduces herself as Maria and tells me that my boyfriend has told her I am a Medium. She requests and offers to pay for a reading. I agree and almost instantly see her grandmother. She is a loving woman from Italy who feels very much like 'a mother' energy. Maria tells me her grandmother raised her. She is also weeping now, and shares she has had a very hard time of it since her grandmother passed eight months back. The grandmother continues to talk about her great grandchildren as well as a reminder to always make her meat sauce; a combination of meatballs, steak and sausage. The reading wraps up after fifteen minutes or so, and Maria is very grateful she was able to hear from her grandmother. I am heartwarmed and hope I have helped bridge a healing between the two sides of the veil.

Maria then tells me a story I will never forget, a story told to her many years ago by the grandmother who just came through. When her grandmother was a little girl living in Sardinia, Italy a great and terrible storm came to the island. The family lived in a house made of stone, perched on a piece of Earth jutted out towards the sea, the head of the island and the place of the first landfall for the impending mammoth storm, a hurricane. Everyone on the island panicked and felt certain that death was coming to some, if not all of them, in what was sure to be tidal waters washing away all that they knew.

The family gathered in the living room, its large windows facing the sea, and prayed. The winds picked up and howled. Salt water sprayed and then pounded at their home. They continued to pray, even more earnestly. The waves started breaking closer to their home. It was just a short time before the ocean washed over them, along with most of their island.

Then, against all reason, her grandfather (the grandfather of Maria's grandmother), quietly got up and walked outside, bracing himself against the immense force of the angry wind. The family cried out begging him to come back. He acted as though he did not hear. He instead stood, as firmly as he could, on a large rock projected determinedly toward the seething ocean. The family watched in horror. His back to them, facing the sea, he threw his arms up and spoke to someone, though the family could not clearly hear his voice. He was pleading with

God or the Sea or both. After a number of minutes, that felt like eternity for the family watching this, they saw much to their disbelief, the ocean roar on either side of this small Italian man; it neither washed him or his home away. It also did not come upon the island but instead chose to travel on either side of it.

The most dangerous part of the storm now passed, the brave man turned and came back into his home. As he was welcomed with hugs and questions, he declined quietly and went into his bedroom and lay there for the next three days; and then died.

“*What do you think about that?*” I asked.

“We did not know what to think about it. It was just an unbelievable story in my family. Unbelievable and yet true.” replied Maria.

“*I think that he made a deal with God, the Sea or Death; probably Death. He traded his one life for the lives of everyone else on the island. He must have been one great Soul to have had enough worth to trade for so much; or an enormous amount of Love.*”

It's dark because you are trying too hard. Lightly child, lightly. Learn to do everything lightly. Yes, feel lightly even though you're feeling deeply. Just lightly let things happen and lightly cope with them. I was so preposterously serious in those days, such a humorless little prig. Lightly, lightly – it's the best advice ever given me. When it comes to dying even. Nothing ponderous, or portentous, or emphatic. No rhetoric, no tremolos, no self conscious persona putting on its celebrated imitation of Christ or Little Nell. And of course, no theology, no metaphysics. Just the fact of dying and the fact of the clear light. So throw away your baggage and go forward. There are quicksands all about you, sucking at your feet, trying to suck you down into fear and self-pity and despair. That's why you must walk so lightly. Lightly my darling, on tiptoes and no luggage, not even a sponge bag, completely unencumbered."

~ Aldous Huxley, Island

Acknowledgements

My deepest gratitude goes to my helpers in the realm of Spirit, who for reasons unbeknownst to me, keep me afloat in every way. It is to them that I dedicate my work as a Medium, since it is only through their help, I am able to do this.

I also want to thank my dear friends Daniel Weaver and Leland Moore who have stood by me and given me so much support and love.

I thank (in no particular order) Angie D'Anjou, Ramona Garcia, Circles of Wisdom, Jo Catalino, Marya Ursin, Laurie Murphy, Karen Silverstine, Stephen Harrington, Norm Moody, Lisa DeLisio, Michael Bergen and Robert Moss.

I have no small debt of gratitude to John McNally who has been witness to my becoming a Medium from that first night at a fundraiser when I was 'tricked' into doing readings, and has always encouraged and supported me. He has promoted me to anyone with an ear, in his own way; with a grand flourish of his arm he exclaims, "May I now introduce you to The Great Morganna!"

Notes:

My ancestor Ouchistauichkoue,(or better known as Marie Sylvestry), for the sake of succinctness, I wrote 'great' twice to denote that she was my grandmother many generations back. The same applies to her father Roch Mantoueabeouichit. Also, records confirm Maries mother Outchibahabanoukoueou was Huron, but some records say her father was Huron and others suspect Abenaki. After my experience meeting my great, great grandfather in Spirit, and he specifically calling the corn he gave me Abenaki, I believe he was of Abenaki descent. Natives married into each other's tribes and my last ancestor to live as a Native was my great grandfather's mother who came from a Mohawk reservation in the early 1900's and married a White farmer in a small town next to Kahnawake in have many Canada.

Canada is remarkable with regard to record keeping and there is a lot of information available regarding Marie and her children. The name Prevost is also associated with her genetic line and I Prevost's on my Mothers line. The best place to do any ancestral research relative to Canada is Laval University in Quebec, where they have an enormous library of records, par excellence.

Index

About The Author

Susan Morgan actively leads workshops on Shamanic Dreamwork in addition to her work as a Medium. More information can be found on her website: **MysticDreamCenter.com.** She is also an artist and resides in beloved New Hampshire. She is the author of ***The Power of Dreams: Tools for Navigating Your Life***, as well ***as The Mystic Dream Journal.***

MYSTIC
DREAM
PUBLISHING HOUSE